Frankie said

CAPP TROTSKY

PAGE PUBLISHING
Conneaut Lake, PA

First originally published by Page Publishing 2023

ISBN 978-1-6624-8296-0 (pbk)
ISBN 978-1-6624-8301-1 (digital)

Printed in the United States of America

I t was a bright and sunny day in Berkeley in the summer of 1968 when Frankie stepped off the Greyhound at University Avenue. He didn't give a thought to what he left behind, only what the future would hold. He was mature for his fourteen years and now free to get his fill of the world his father tried so hard to protect him from.

Freedom. That is what he craved. He breathed in the free air. He looked around at the unremarkable but bustling west of campus business district that is San Pablo Avenue and University. He threw the bag of clothes over his shoulder and headed up University toward "The Ave," Telegraph Avenue.

He heard about The Ave from Andy Albee, older brother of Robbie and Candy, friends of Frankie's. He was among the first to experience what was happening there. Andy was the oldest of the Albee Clan. There were about ten Albees, charming people. Both mom and dad had kind of turned up noses. You could always tell an Albee. Dad was a minister (of some sort) and never around. They called him Mr. Nitty. He didn't care what the kids did anyway, so everyone hung out at their house. Andy was a singer in a rock band. They did Vanilla Fudge and Spirit songs, and they were good. Andy's light shows were unsurpassed, ahead of their time.

Of course, by now, the Haight Ashbury was being called The Hate. "Don't come" was the message. The message was "go to The Ave."

People's Park—Itchycoo Park by The Small Faces, that's where Frankie was headed. He would get high and touch the sky. He would grow his hair down to his ass. He wanted to be hip; he wanted to belong, just like everybody else did. He wanted to be a hippie, but his dad wouldn't let him grow his hair out, the prick.

Bobby Kennedy and Martin Luther King were assassinated, the riots at the Democratic National Convention in Chicago happened, the Tet Offensive, worldwide antiwar demonstrations occurred as a result of the Vietnam War, and the Summer Olympics was a disaster as the world watched the first live telecast from outer space. The year rocked the world.

Only as he got near the UC Berkeley campus did he start seeing student types (with long hair) whom he could start asking to see if any of them had a place for him to crash. He was uncertain about what to say and how to act when asking someone if he could crash at their pad. He better just get to The Ave and take a look around.

In a new world with more history than he was used to seeing, the UC Berkeley campus showed its age. He didn't really know what he was looking at though. He was looking for, looking for… He didn't know what he was looking for. He was getting away from one thing he knew he had to get away from and hadn't had time to think about where he was going. And here it was, all before him, right up the street.

As he walked up Bancroft Street, he didn't see anything defining the new culture or anything. A Free Huey sign and Free Bobby Seal were the new signs of revolt, Black Power. No sign of antiwar demonstrators. It was pretty quiet. Zak from the Lovin' Spoonful was holding court on the steps of the plaza, but they were more self-absorbed than interested in sharing too widely the inside scoop with everyone around. Maybe it wasn't fit for the student body.

Lots of people with long hair so he was getting warm. He expected more action in terms of protests with angry students (who actually had a good reason to be angry) and that sort of thing, but it was reduced to a nice day in a college town with people going about their business. It had been ten hours since he slit the screen in his bedroom window at his father's house in Sacramento, jumped out, and made it to the bus station. It was time to look for a place to stay.

Finally a tall guy with shoulder-length curly brown hair, unshaven, wearing Ivy League loafers with no socks, took mercy on Frankie and said, "My roommates out of town. This way." He didn't give a name, ask questions, or want to know anything about who Frankie was or where he was from or what was he doing there. The guy had a typical apartment (built in the '30s) just up from the North Gate with the spare bedroom. There was, of course, no food in the equation. Food really didn't matter. Single mattress on the floor with Indian print bedspread, wooden box next to the bed—neat. It was a female roommate, he could tell. Things were tidy, and incense had been burned.

"I'll wake you up early," said the guy and closed the door and left him. He felt safe for the moment. Not that he felt threatened; he was wide-eyed and not sure which way was up. He acted like he knew what was going on, as much as anybody else did know what was going on. Frankie made a break for freedom as he then found it necessary. He had to get away from the overwhelming domination of his father and didn't have to think too much how or why he was where he was. He was excited about being where he was. It was the first day of freedom. It was a good day.

He had a normal middle-class upbringing filled with activities of a normal American family. Baseball preoccupied his time, and the San Francisco Giants were his favorite team. His dad was either coach or manager of all his Little League teams except one that he was selected by a famous retired big-league player whose teams won. He was picked by the Cardinals while his dad managed the Yankees. He would have been a big fish in a little pond had he gone to the Yankees; with the Cards, he was a little fish.

In the reality of Berkeley in 1968, he was a very little fish, not even a mouthful. Not that he realized that. He didn't know much of anything, but he was tired and slept.

He was at attention when awakened. The sun was shining; it was a new day. Next thing he knew he was walking back across campus with the guy whose pad he had crashed at, and before the fellow turned into a big building that had to be his morning class, he said, "Go to the Free Church up on Durant."

"Thanks," said Frankie.

"Where's Durant?" Frankie asked a guy moving up the plaza in a studious manner with some hair.

"That way," he replied, pointing down The Ave.

Frankie was about to get his first look at what everyone was talking about. The Ave was where it was at. The culture, the revolution, the social phenomena unfolding at the right time for Frankie—not that he had a choice about that. Was he the lucky one that he was there then? Was it a blessed time, or was he cursed to be wandering into the time and space he was wandering into? And he hadn't even taken acid yet. Down The Ave he headed; it was getting interesting.

Frankie was all eyes as he walked down the street. He mostly encountered older and sort of downtrodden types, asking Frankie for money. That was funny; he didn't have any money.

The angry "Free Huey" posters were abundant. "Kill the Pigs!" "Stop the Draft!" were signs left in the gutter, leaning on buildings. There were real reasons to be pissed off. There was excitement in the air. Trouble was brewing, and Frankie was on his way to the Free Church. Sure enough, right off The Ave in a rundown Victorian was the Free Church. Scruffy kids and older hippies alike hung around the front, inside the entry throughout the first-floor rooms, up the stairs, hanging around, waiting, or killing time.

"If you're waiting to see Reverend Richard, there's nothing he can do for runaways," said a kid who saw that Frankie was but one of many who flocked to The Ave to be part of the same thing the people sitting on the steps had.

Frankie didn't realize he was so obvious. Lots of cigarette smoking and some chess playing were preoccupying most of those hanging out.

Then a door opened from an upstairs room, and out came Reverend Richard. A mass of frizzed-out blond hair, full-length purple velvet robe, and a collar. He was the original hip priest. He took the next person waiting in the office and closed the door.

So Frankie realized he was in the same boat as everybody else and found a step to sit down on. From the step, he got into a chess game and some cigarette smoking.

Eventually, he met an older guy (probably twenty-five) who kind of took an interest in him, Ray. Ray was hanging around and apparently had aspirations to become a priest also, or at least wear a collar, a mail-order collar. It got a reaction, carried some weight.

Ray had a '65 red Falcon station wagon; his mom owned a couple of houses Twenty-Seventh Street in Oakland, off The Ave. He lived in one. Frankie just sort of tagged along with this kind of lonely social outcast who wanted to belong, like everybody else, and Frankie was his new sounding board. He vocalized, and Frankie listened about this and that. Frankie was all ears. Ray painted houses and did maintenance for a property management company in Oakland, when he worked. But now it was time to get experienced.

The year 1968 was the year of *Bullitt*, with Steve McQueen; *2001: A Space Odyssey* ("Open the pod door, Hal"); *Planet of the Apes*, Charlton Heston; *Beggars Banquet*, the Rolling Stones; *The White Album*, the Beatles; *Cheap Thrills*, Big Brother and the Holding Company with Janis Joplin; *Born to Be Wild* by Steppenwolf. Frankie was listening carefully. What a time to be born.

"Here, have a real cigarette," Ray said to Frankie. He was glad to get a factory-rolled cancer even though he had become an expert hand roller of the street variety. In response to Ray's monologue, Frankie had nothing to say, but he was working on it. He'd say something sooner or later other than "Ah, I guess." He was, after all, a child, about to learn the ways of the world that he so boldly threw himself into a few days before. He could hardly care less who got assassinated for whatever reason. It was all right with him as long as his hair got long.

Ray's house was old and dingy without furniture. A young long-haired kid was a house quest, who was only seen lying in a sleeping bag on the hardwood dining room floor, always reading a very engrossing paperback that he could not tear himself away from, especially to acknowledge the presence of others. Ignoring him was the order of the day and every day to come. Frankie may have been lacking when it came to participating in any kind of dialogue, but he was listening to Ray's jabber.

Ray was good enough to buy him dinner at a local restaurant then handed him a tiny blue pill and said, "Take this." Frankie, without question, popped it in his mouth.

"Oh, wow," he might have said. He didn't know whether he said it or just thought it. Was he stoned? So they were in Ray's bedroom, which was furnished enough to sit and listen to KMPX. Frankie's education was about to begin. Ray was not gay, but being hip meant you had to be gay too. It was kind of like wearing a collar. He was kind of licking his lips with the acid experimentation one does with their face before they go into the bathroom to look in the mirror to make sure: "Yep, I'm stoned."

Frankie was stoned on acid. That was maximum adult dosage (250 mics) of Blue Cheer—"Ain't no Cure for the Summertime Blues." A potentially life-changing dosage and not a clue what he had just taken. Many ended up in mental institutions as a result of not knowing the punch the seemingly harmless little pill packed. He was lucky to be in a safe environment and about to be guided through his trip with the help of those playing all night music for those like Frankie who were up all night stoned on acid.

Jimi Hendrix, Cream, Canned Heat, Country Joe, and the Fish. Wow, this was really something, Frankie began to realize.

Yeah, this was good—if you survived it, Frankie thought. His eyes were open now, and lookee here, everybody was on it, everybody hip. *We are all one.*

Frankie tagged along with Ray for a while, scraping peeling paint on a house or two. Hanging around the Free Church was the primary pastime.

Not that Frankie gave a shit, but Lyndon Johnson, who was the president they hated, would not run for another term, but he got word that Richard Nixon was running, and they really hated him—those of them that were hip. They all had the same political views. Demonstrations against the war in Vietnam taking place in Berkeley and throughout the country on college campuses were happening; there was much strife.

The My Lai massacre, where soldiers killed innocent civilians, was a battle cry against the war. War was wrong; it gave the rallying cry to the discontent. Frankie was watching but not reacting to that. It was war. He didn't think there could be rules to war. He was a dumb kid. What did he know? Nothing. But the Beatles sang about love, so that's what he wanted too.

When Detroit and many other cities burned, James Brown, the God Father of Soul himself, appealed to the community to stop the violence. He was trashed and accused of being a tool for whitey. Better not say that, brother. Frankie didn't know anything about prejudice, but he was learning. Whatever side he had to be on to be hip was the side he was on. Whatever politics having long hair meant was the side he was on. So much for baseball—nothing hip about that.

If the '60s hadn't come along, Frankie would probably have gone on to play professional baseball. He was the best player in his league. All they did as kids was play baseball. So much for that. Now he was taking acid. He was tuning in, turning on, and dropping out, just like Timothy Leary said to do.

Hanging around the Free Church, Frankie met Dak. He was a student at CAL taking chemistry, learning Russian, and other heady subjects. He played chess and had Frankie over to his apartment on Ellsworth in Berkeley. It was a bad pad. Books, tapestries, good sound system, art, a cat—very cool. Frankie wanted this life. Styling. A man of the world. Incense was burned (the good kind, rock); the best kief was smoked. Dak was the tip of the spear.

Dak sneered at the bad-smelling Ray (Frankie never noticed) and his phony collar. He also took a genuine and stand-up regard for Frankie and got Reverend Richard to take notice of this one. Together they gave Frankie the responsible talking to that persuaded him to return home and finish school like everyone was supposed to do and then come back and become a member of the revolution, for the greater good and all that.

Frankie did the right thing they all thought and called Betty, his mom. Betty was one husband number three, a retired navy admiral, he said. He had a bunch of cool model ships, so he might have been a real navy guy, but he was kind of a weiner. He had a daughter who was a real stoner and out of the picture mostly. She and her boyfriend were off somewhere taking lots of acid, she said. She could certainly talk the talk.

"Frankie, where are you? We were worried sick about you. I thought you were dead in a ditch somewhere. How could you do that to me?" said Betty.

The Oakland Police were present when Ed and Betty picked Frankie up from a safe house Ray managed in the Oakland Hills.

"How could you call the Oakland Pigs?" Frankie yelled at them when he was at the back of Ed's gold '67 Mustang. They looked at each other with a long gaze as if to say, "Oh shit." Trouble was the order of the day.

That was the beginning of the time they would have for the next couple of months—lucky for all Frankie thought. He didn't realize how good he had it. This was a tolerant mother and her "yes, dear" husband. Admirals are kind of pussies anyway, even militarily. Frankie knew nothing from nothing, and that added up to nothing. He was a throbbing piece of meat, poor boy. So he was now in the care, or custody, of Betty and Ed. He was in high school, taking the smart kid classes at Kennedy High. New to him. He didn't know anybody, and that was the way he liked it. He was doing his time. Betty, who smoked cigarettes, let him smoke. He smoked a pipe. He read Greek Mythology and astrology; he was an intellectual. Silk Indian tapestries (like Dak's from Berkeley) hung from the ceiling of his room. Johnny Winter, Savoy Brown, and early Punk were played on his stereo, early Punk.

He was a good student and an artist, something Betty encouraged in his childhood. He exhibited a talent for it. She took him to private art lessons when he was but a child. He did his first oil painting when he was eight.

Betty was ill-equipped to handle her own problems, let alone understand the problems of a young boy. She was still a child when she had him, eighteen. She wasn't about to let on that she didn't know much. She was cursed with people telling her she was pretty. It went straight to her head. She could do no wrong. She became a model and taught modeling professionally.

The boy was too smart to be given answers like "because I said so." When asking for his allowance for doing household chores (so he could buy pipe tobacco), she said, "I'll give it to you when I'm ready." Bitch.

He was listening to music in the living room, tapping his foot to "Rollin' and Tumblin'" by Johnny Winter. She was not done with him and came in to give him a piece of her mind and said, "Turn that down!"

"I'll turn it down when I'm ready," said the insolent little prick. She got so pissed off by the indignant statement she couldn't help but start smacking the shit out of him sitting on the couch. That he was laughing surely pissed her off even more, and as he covered up his head to deflect the attempted open-handed slaps that, of course, he desperately deserved, she fell over him and hit her head on a picture frame above the couch on the wall and cut her head. She was bleeding.

As if choreographed, Ed entered the room wielding a club and, in a shaking fit, seeing his wife having been assaulted by this smart-ass kid, began hitting Frankie with the club. He was probably deserving of the beating he was getting, but the Admiral was connecting with a few of these blows. Frankie had to overcome the smaller man and throw him through the TV. It was time for Frankie to leave. Frankie grabbed a few things and headed for the river.

He knew some French hippies who lived around the corner from the Albee's. For some reason, he went to their house. He didn't know them that well. Chad, the younger brother, and Wick, the older brother. Chad Chadwick and Wick Chadwick. Their mom was wild-looking, with a glass eye she would lose from time to time. They'd find it on the closet floor looking up at them once in a while. She drank wine all day. They also had a frequent guest by the name of Digger, who had a mass of blond curly hair and played the harp. Their yard was weeds with crap all over the place. They were real hippies, in Sacramento.

Even though they lived by the Albee's, Frankie knew them through some wild French kid he went to Einstein Junior High in Rosemont with and participated in a little juvenile delinquency, Gary Applegate. He had an older brother who knew Digger. They were thieving little shits. Gary had a Chevy pass key, and they ended up stealing a couple cars to take joy riding. They were two blocks from his dad's house when a motorcycle cop spotted them in a stolen '57 Chevy and pulled them over for making a wrong turn or something.

Frankie's dad, Arnie, just about strangled him when he picked him up from juvy that night, in the later part of 1967. "I ought to kill you, you little son of a bitch!" he screamed with gritting teeth inches from Frankie's face in the front seat of the car with a couple of fistfuls of the kid's jacket. Frankie looked him in the eye and said, "Go ahead!" He realized he couldn't kill the little bastard, let him go, and drove home.

The Chadwicks were good for a night, but he had to get to Gary's, who lived in a nearby subdivision, Rosemont. Arnie was aware of where Gary lived and, more importantly, where Peter lived. Peter was Frankie's best friend and had been for years. Peter lived right around the corner from Gary.

Rosemont was a nice place with nice people. Around the other corner was Randy's house. Randy was a couple years older than Frankie and Peter. He had a black light in his bedroom with psyche-delic posters, a job (he was a mechanic), a VW bus (with curtains), a pool, and a totally cool mom, Lois. Frankie moved right in. He loved them, and they loved him. It was the summer of 1969, and it was time to party.

Not only did Frankie's best friend Peter live around the corner, a welfare mother with a bunch of kids, most importantly teenage girls, moved in down the street from Randy from Topanga Canyon. They were big Taj Mahal fans (also from Topanga). *Giant Step* came out about then. Great record.

Frankie, Peter, Randy, and the teenage girls, Elaine (the one they all had the hots for) and Rosie, her sister, spent a lot of time in Randy's bus listening to the eight-track—Creedence Clearwater Revival, the Steve Miller Band, and of course, Led Zeppelin.

While Randy was at work, Peter and Frankie frequented the pool. They were floating on air mattresses looking up at the moon one night, and Frankie said, "Imagine that there are people walking on the moon right now."

It was the summer of '69, and their hair was getting long and they were getting tan. John Mayall's *Turning Point* was their favorite album. "Room to Move" was recorded live at Albert Hall. He made the jewelry jingle with that one. Yet he dressed in Indian garb by the campfire and lived in some canyon. That's what they wanted to do too.

On the Fourth of July, Frankie snuck up to the backyard of Arnie's house and freed Kelly, his dog. Kelly was his fully trained (by him) devoted Irish setter. It killed him having to leave her there when he ran around trying to get a front-row seat in the cultural fun ride. He knew she would be in good hands with Arnie when he was off seeking freedom. They ran toward the river. They were free.

Frankie, Kelly, Peter, his out-of-control Doberman Cher, their camping gear, and a few weeks' worth of food (kindly paid for by his father) piled in Peter's dad's '64 Valiant and headed for the hills. Peter's dad was an older gentleman not good at coping with a couple of rambunctious dogs, but they made it. He dropped them off in a remote high mountain river in the Sierras, where they became one with nature. They became a couple of little Indians with no need for the outside world.

They did finally come out to restock and relocate. Thank goodness Peter's dad was willing to foot the bill and transport them all over California. He and the wife (also an older woman) preferred to sit quietly and read with their toy lapdogs. They didn't want the commotion of teenage kids and rowdy dogs disturbing their peace.

The boys needed some action, some girls to look at. They wouldn't quite know what to do with one if they actually caught the attention of one (teenage girl). They were wary of how aggressive girls their age were when it came to "doing it." Not sure they were ready. But they liked to watch.

They relocated to Pinecrest Lake, in Tuolumne County, next to Strawberry, on the way to Yosemite, where there was some action. They found the perfect rock on which to set up camp on the other side of the lake from the lodge and the boat ramp, campground, and teenage girls. They met a hip chick from Oakdale their age, whom Frankie became rather smitten with, who wanted to be a hippie too. She embroidered and did feminine arsty-craftsy stuff he liked. She had to leave sooner than she wanted (with her parents probably) but would carry on a romance by the US mail that would last for years.

Woodstock happened without Frankie and Peter hearing much about it. No TV, no radio—they didn't exactly read the paper, if the lodge even got one.

The boys were without dope of any kind; cigarettes were all they had. One night they were sitting around the campfire with a couple of other kids and their dogs when the local California Highway Patrol officer named Fat Albert showed up and decided to search everyone. Of course the dogs were barking, and Fat Albert said, "I'm going to Mace those dogs if you don't shut 'em up!" They got tied to some tree roots. Fat Albert was shining his flashlight into a Marlboro box that maybe had a little tobacco in the bottom of it and said, "Yep, sure looks like marajuanie to me!" His sidekick, Lester, turned around to take a look, and Frankie, who was standing a few feet away, bolted into the trees. Lester was hot on his trail with his flashlight beam bouncing around the trees everywhere but where Frankie was. He was getting away, so Lester fired a couple of shots. Bullets were hitting the tree branches hanging near Frankie as he ran for his life. He was, after all, a runaway.

Frankie made his way back through the forest close enough to the campsite to see what was going on. Fat Albert guessed correctly that the threat of shooting Kelly would get Frankie to turn himself in and pulled out his gun and aimed it at the dog. "No, don't, don't!" he yelled as he walked into camp with his hands up.

They put Frankie in a jail used since the gold rush in Sonora for a week. The Sacramento Pigs finally came an hour before the Tuolumne County Sheriff was going to let him go because they had already held him for a week.

In Sacramento Juvenile Detention Facility, they gave him a court date, three weeks from then at 11:00 a.m. Three weeks later, at 11:00 a.m., the judge said, "You'll be here in juvenile detention with us for thirty days." They put him back in a cell, only to return him to the courtroom where a very irritated Arnie, who had missed the previous proceedings because he had been told 1:00 p.m., was causing a ruckus. The judge said, "Okay, okay, Mr. Thomas, please relax. I'll release him into your custody under one condition—that he get a haircut."

That was not the only condition, though. He would be put on probation.

Mr. Neptune was the least qualified individual to have authority over anyone, let alone high school students considered problem kids who met once a week after school.

Neptune's most valuable words of wisdom to them one day was "when I was a kid and stepped out of line, my dad would knuckle my head." He would then make a fist next to his head and turn it in a quick twisting motion. "My brother makes ten thousand dollars a year more than I do. I just wish he'da started knuckling sooner." He was a real Pencil Neck. He said, "I've never lost a boy." That was when Frankie got a reason.

Frankie was not liking the new rule of law Arnie, Joni (the evil stepmother), and Neptune were imposing—not that he could do anything about it.

He made contact with Dak, who came from Berkeley in his baby-blue '67 Mustang. Neptune showed up to get a look and give him a grilling. "What's your full name?" he asked.

"Daniel Andres Kildare."

"Where do you live?"

"Berkeley."

"What's your address?"

"It's 2336 Ellsworth." He was totally forthcoming, except the address was bogus. When they were walking to the car, Dak said to Frankie, "I see what you mean. You gotta get outta here. In the meantime…" He reached into the car and from a stash spot found a small package which he quietly slipped to Frankie. "This will make it a bit more tolerable until you do."

When Dak was off to Berkeley, Frankie examined the care package. Blue double barrels (Blue Cheer, 250 mics), ten hits, 1/8 ounce of kief. Nice.

Frankie was doing his time, not making it too rough on himself. Arnie was a ballbuster. Joni was taking full advantage of her new-found power over him. He couldn't hold out anymore when a major concert was scheduled in central California with several top bands. Peter said, "We can't miss this. We're going in Randy's bus." Elaine,

Rosie, Peter, Randy, and Cathy (Randy's girlfriend) were leaving early Friday morning.

When he got home, he asked if he could go to the concert, to which Arnie said, "No." That's what he figured he'd say, but Frankie wasn't going to let that stop him. Friday morning, he was ready to go to a party.

The VW bus with curtains bounced and rolled on down the road, full. The eight-track was playing Blind Faith's "I Can't Find My Way Home."

Frankie met up with Patrice, and the group made their way into position in front of the stage. Taj Mahal, Sons of Chaplin, Ike and Tina Turner, Country Joe and the Fish, James Cotton, and many others were playing. It was a two-day concert.

That night Frankie popped Patrice's cherry right there in the middle of the standing crowd in a sleeping bag on the ground. They were all stoned on acid, so it was the most natural thing in the world to do. It was a wonderful experience until the Hell's Angels decided to ride their bikes through the middle of the crowd and scare the shit out of everybody. Darkness was descending on a culture based on peace and love. Tomorrow Frankie was about to face another darkness. "You're grounded for a month!" Arnie said as Frankie walked in.

"Yeah, I know, I know!" Frankie said and retreated to his room. Frankie was back in high school (Hiram Johnson) with a renewed purpose—for education anyway. With an expanded awareness, he now appreciated higher learning. Without telling him, his friend Brent (some friend) dropped a hit of acid in his milk at lunch one day. Frankie thought he was going mad in the first period after lunch, English class. The teacher took on a reptilian demeanor, and English didn't make much sense. The frosty greenish-blue shadowy hue on things and vibrating wavelengths of life force distracted him that day. Dinner with Arnie and Joni was interesting. He had come down enough to be paranoid, but they didn't have a clue. He was an experienced astral traveler at sixteen.

Arnie and Frankie were doing the required yard work when a neighbor of theirs, who was kind of a cool jock type (and happened to be a probation officer. Why couldn't Frankie get a guy like that for a PO?), asked Frankie, "Going to see the Stones at Altamont?" He looked at Arnie's face and said, "No."

Altamont was the Stone's way of making up for having missed Woodstock. The Hell's Angels killed a guy and generally cast an ugly vibe onto the scene. They roughed up Jagger, who deserved it for being stupid enough to hire them for security. Frankie was bummed that he missed it. Dak, however, was there, and with his expensive camera equipment, he got what turned out to be a famous picture of Jagger taking a swig of a bottle of Jack Daniels. The era of love and peace was over. It really only took a few years to get ugly.

There was no particular straw that broke the camel's back. Arnie, Joni, and Neptune were such a group of assholes that Frankie, even with his newfound maturity and patience, could not endure. He had to get out.

This time there would be no fooling around. He would have to leave for good and prove to them, and to himself, his independence.

Brent, Frankie's good buddy (the one that put acid in his milk without telling him), whose ass he should have kicked, well, Frankie forgave him. He had a '64 Mercury Comet that had made the trip to Berkeley once before, to Dak's.

"Brent, can you give me a ride to Berkeley tonight? I gotta get outta here."

"Sure Frankie, let me tell Sarah" (his girlfriend…adventurous). She would want to come along for the ride and what she was going to see in Berkeley.

By now, Dak had made a lot of money dealing acid and lived in a fabulous pad, with a full top-of-the-line Macintosh stereo system, amp, receiver, indictor, preamp—a thing of beauty. Monster Altec Lansing, the original egg-shaped stereo listening chair. He had the best of everything that money could buy, in the way of toys.

"I knew it was just a matter of time. I don't know how you held out for so long," said Dak as they crossed the threshold into the living room.

"I hate leaving Kelly behind. She'll be all right there, I guess.

"I had no idea you had to go away and think you couldn't come here. That it was that bad," said Dak. He got the story from Frankie about the adventures away from home after he was in Berkeley and he, Dak, and Reverend Richard, convinced Frankie to return home and "stick it out." Not that it was ever more than verbal abuse; it was too oppressive in a time when there was such a need for freedom.

"We have to be sure not to let Neptune catch up with you," Dak said with a big smile.

They got comfortable on the luxurious couch and chairs and passed the pipe around with some exquisite Afgany hash and tripped out on the art. Brent and Sarah had to go back to Sacramento. Time to take some acid.

Frankie knew Dak was gay. It seemed that it was part of being hip. He had not had any homosexual relations yet. Dak was taking his time priming this one for what he had in mind. He took Frankie clothes shopping and bought him some things. Then to see *I Am Curious (Yellow)*, some French film of some not very attractive broad getting fucked in all kinds of public places in Paris. So what. Not much of a thrill. He first gave him some acid and then took him to a fancy Russian restaurant in San Francisco for dinner. Frankie couldn't seem to chew his food and swallow it. They had to get their expensive dinners to go.

That evening Dak had Frankie in a trance. The time had come for Frankie to learn what it meant to be hip. They were sitting on the couch, stoned on acid, smoking hash, drinking wine, and had just finished their food to go. It was time he learned what it meant to be hip. Dak unzipped his pants and began sucking his dick.

Not feeling quite right about what was happening, Frankie kept quiet. Finally, he felt the uncontrollable urge to pee and couldn't hold it. Noticing that Dak was sucking more feverishly, he let himself explode in Dak's mouth. Frankie got his first nut. But why would this guy want to drink it? It wasn't something Frankie wanted to do if that's what it meant to be gay or hip or either. That would be the extent of Frankie's education for now. Dak was moving slowly. He didn't want to freak him out with too much, too soon, like fucking him in the ass.

With Neptune possibly hot on Frankie's trail, having interrogated Dak in Sacramento and gotten information from him about his location, factual or fictional, it was time to relocate. Frankie moved in with Reverend Richard and his hot wife. They lived in a modest house off Solano in Albany. As it turned out, even with a hot wife, Reverend Richard was also gay and wanted a little taste of Frankie. Was being gay a requirement for being hip?

This time Frankie resisted Richard when they ended up one night at the Free Church offices. "I don't want to do this," Frankie said.

Getting his dick sucked was one thing; holding and kissing was not something Frankie wanted to do with anyone other than Patrice, a female. Richard didn't force the issue.

Even though he ended up with a couple of pervs, they had his best interest at heart (really…strange but true) and decided the best course of action was for Frankie to get out of Berkeley. The first order of business was a name change with a nice new driver's license. Frankie wasn't old enough to worry about the draft, but he was about to be. Those dodging the draft had created the need for things such as phony ID, and Dak knew where to get it. "So where would you like to go? What city?" Since he knew Dak used to live in Boston, he said, "Boston." He bought Frankie a winter coat, gave him a hundred bucks, and a ride to the airport.

Frankie got off the plane at Logan Airport. Bbbrrrrr… It was colder than he had felt before. *Five degrees…what have I done?* he thought. He had the address for a drop-in center similar to the Free Church that could help him get situated. Not only was it colder than shit, the South End (of Boston) was a war zone. He had never seen a real ghetto before. It was ugly.

In the deepest, darkest coldest part of the remaining brick structures not in ruin was the Guiding Light. It was not an inviting place, but within were young people with long hair, and they knew the way around. "I'm looking for a place to stay and a job," said Frankie to the young woman sitting at a desk upon which a phone sat, which was ringing. She answered the phone with a disgusted look on her face for having to answer the same stupid question a hundred times. She hung up and said, "Ask around. That guy over there is looking for a place too. Maybe you can get together." She pointed out an older guy with long hair and a long handlebar mustache talking to some kids.

"I'm looking for a place. I hear you are too," Frankie said to the guy.

"You got any money?" he asked.

"Yeah," said Frankie.

"New York Bob," he said, holding out his hand.

"Frankie."

"Where you from, Frankie?" he asked.

"San Francisco."

"San Francisco Frank, eh?"

"Yeah."

"Haight and Clayton used to be my corner. I sold the *Free Press* and the *Barb*." Bob was a recognizable image that had been beamed all over the world as one of the faces of "the hippies" in the Haight Ashbury, standing there with long hair and the long mustache, no shirt, standing on the corner holding up copies of The *Barb* and The *Free Press*. Frankie was lucky to have hooked up with Bob, he knew things.

They got a room together on the low-rent side of Beacon Hill. Bob got a job washing dishes, and Frankie got a job at a cannery in Brookline. On his first day, Frankie was told to "go find Bonnie and see what he wants you to do."

"Okay. Is Bonnie around?" he asked a guy working there.

"Ova thea."

He walked around the Hawaiian Punch/HIC Fruit Punch cannery asking for Bonnie. He finally was directed to the right guy. "You Bonnie?" he asked.

"Yeah, I'm Bonnie," said the smallish middle-aged guy. On his shirt was the name "Barney."

They routinely ate at Beacon Chambers. Beacon Chambers was a residential hotel and a restaurant on top of Beacon Hill that catered to the large population of mostly older and mostly gross men. One night Frankie was having some apple pie with ice cream. Bob was in the room sipping Southern Comfort. "What'er you? Some kinda hippie or somethun? We don't like long hairs around here," said a nondescript but angry, scruffy dude. When Frankie got back to the room, he mentioned the incident to Bob, who flew into a rage. "I'll kill the motherfucker, let's go," he said and was out the door. Frankie spotted the guy and also noticed that Bob had a knife out, ready to carve up some redneck ass.

"He's not here," said Frankie. Before the words left his mouth, Bob had the guy in his clutches and was whacking away on him. A few days later, Bob and Frankie were walking down Myrtle Street and came upon the guy on crutches and all bandaged up. He fell down, backing away, having dropped his crutches, and pleaded, "Please don't hurt me. I'm sorry, I'm sorry."

Bob leaned over him and said, "Don't ever fuck with hippies again."

"Okay, okay," said the guy.

The job shoveling one scoop of white powder (sugar) and one scoop red powder (punch flavor) into big tanks late at night to early in the morning was just too grueling. He would never drink HI C or Hawaiian Punch again. He got a job at a bookbindery for a US investor. He was doing grunt work handling the paper scraps and melting down lead type. It was a pretty good job, actually. It was in downtown Boston. Frankie had been there for a couple months, and the guy in charge invited Frankie into his office. "You could get in on the ground floor and a great business opportunity with this company." Frankie foolishly moved on to something else.

He and Bob would part ways. Frankie got a room in a nice old building on Myrtle Street. It was a two-hundred-year-old building with a charming landlady with whom we would eat cheese and crackers and drink wine with. Also in the place lived an aspiring musician named Ray who thought Bob Dylan was just the greatest songwriter ever and played his songs. He played guitar and sang himself. They made friends with a young couple from Michigan who lived downstairs in one of the really nice apartments. They were students with strong political views. They smoked pot. Frankie and Ray hung out with them.

It became apparent that the area was thick with perverts. A gross old man who lived behind them stood in front of the window, beating the meat, looking at them. They called him Jack Off. He was one of many, especially with Beacon Chambers right up the street.

The shootings at Kent State were a rallying cry that would unite the youth of the nation against the war against the government. "Tin soldiers and Nixon coming, we're finally on our own, four dead in O-hi-o."

One day Frankie was reading the *Boston Globe* and came across an article about a couple of seminary students who started a church-sponsored drop-in center and drug hotline. There were pictures of the two fellows, and Frankie liked one who had long hair and a Hitler mustache. Through the affiliated church, he made contact with the guy.

"I used to work at the Free Church of Berkeley. I have experience working with kids on drugs. I know all about it." That was pretty much the truth too. He had taken acid about fifty times and survived it. He knew the difference between where one's personality and identity began and ended and the effects of the drug and how extreme expanded awareness of what was already there would affect what was already there. No big deal. He had read Leary's book, Alpert's book, Watt's books. He knew what he was talking about. He knew how to come back from a bad acid trip. Reality itself was twisted and would change his view later, but at the time, he believed he was invincible.

"Meet me at my place in Cambridge, and we'll talk," said Tom, the idea guy seminary student, artist, and sculptor. "At 3387 Central, a couple blocks from Central Square, five o'clock," he said.

"Okay."

It was an interesting, funny triangular storefront he had turned into an artist studio and a dark dungeon basement for sleeping, away from street noise. Boston and Cambridge were a series of squares (or squaaes), which had a rotary, and all the streets went directly straight away in a sunburst pattern, like spokes of a wheel, creating all these goofy angles—pregrid.

"Have a seat. Would you like some chamomile tea?" he asked.

"That'd be great, thanks," said Frankie.

"So you have experience in crisis work with kids?" Tom said.

"Yeah, I have experience in talking people through bad trips and am a psychology student. Cal Berkeley."

"Is that right?" He sat down and poured a couple cups of tea. "How old are you?"

"Eighteen. Wanna see my ID?"

"No, that's okay. So you think you can be a drug counselor, right?" asked Tom.

"You need someone like me who's been through it and knows what they're going through," said Frankie.

"We're just getting started. We have a storefront on Mount Auburn Street that we're working on. Why don't you come down tomorrow and meet the others and see what we're doing?"

"Sounds good," said Frankie.

Frankie showed up to find several long-haired young people, and not so young, working to transform what was just a dingy old storefront into a drop-in center for young people in crisis. Like Berkeley, Cambridge was a college town. The storefront was a block away from Harvard Square. And like Berkeley, kids from all over New England and beyond were flocking to where it was at to belong. Be part of the revolution. Run away from home; take acid.

Sanctuary was created as a drop-in center for kids who would show up, usually at the Cambridge Common, across from campus. In those days, for some reason, kids didn't consider what they were going to eat or where they were going to stay. No money. No problem. Somebody would feed you. You didn't worry.

The other seminary student was a lawyer who did fundraising. Mostly hitting up the Episcopal and Catholic churches, which were rich and had resources. It was enough for them to live comfortably. Frankie moved from Beacon Hill to the rent-free accommodations at the Episcopal Theological Seminary on Brattle Street just outside Harvard Square into a nice apartment. Being a graduate school, the people who were attending ETS were often married, so they were built (way back when) to furnish such a living situation, the well-heeled future Episcopal priests. Very few of the people who attended ETS lived in the high-class apartments in the dormitory, so Frankie almost had the place to himself. Peter Lund and his wife and Dick Gresel and his wife lived in the dormitory and also ended up with senior positions at Sanctuary. They were both kind of straight, even though they had long hair and looked the part, but they were Ivy League squares.

There was an assortment of people of different ages with varying skills. Some were psychology students that became Sanctuary staff—paid staff. There were a lot of volunteers who did part-time work in addition to being students. Frankie was glad to have gotten in on the ground floor.

Half of the storefront was an office with desks with phones to be a hotline for anyone in trouble (like a bad acid trip) or some kind of service that maybe they could refer the caller to. A staff member had to be there at all times. They were reasonably trained to handle most emergencies. The other half was platforms covered in carpet to hang out on and even sleep. That Harvard owned everything the Catholic and Episcopal church's didn't made it possible to have a hostel and even serve food in the otherwise unused beautiful buildings. It was made clear what Sanctuary's agenda was. It was not sympathetic to the establishment or "the system." Frankie was right at home.

Just before he moved into ETS, Frankie and Ray went to see Ten Years After at the Band Shell at the park on the Charles River. They had already seen BB King and Janis Joplin. Ray met a college girl who was a little nymph and could not seem to get enough. She was always coming around. With all the loving going on, Frankie felt compelled to get some too.

When the concert was over, the crowd was shuffling toward the exit. Frankie spotted a beauty and said, "You wanna smoke a joint?" He didn't have anything else to say, nor did he have a joint, but Ray did.

"Yeah, all right," she said.

"Can I bum a joint?" Frankie pleaded with Ray.

"What's your name?" she asked.

"Frankie."

"Hi, I'm Paula." She was the most beautiful creature he had ever laid eyes on—long brown hair, beautiful brown eyes, perfect body, and thank God, had some social skills. At least she was engaging him. "My car is over there." Wow, she had a car. They walked to the car and smoked a joint. She was eighteen.

Frankie told her he was eighteen too. "Wanna do something tomorrow?" he asked.

"Okay, I'll meet you at the common tomorrow."

The next day Frankie was waiting at the Boston Common, and there she was. She had on a thin red blouse that had two pouches in which her perfect perky breasts bounced without a bra. What a beauty, what a babe. He was beginning to realize what life was for.

They spent the day walking around downtown Boston. "I had a really nice day," she said.

"Me too," said Frankie. He didn't know what came next. "Can I call you?" he asked.

They went their separate ways. Frankie was at Tom's when she called. "Can I come over? I really want to see you."

"Yeah sure."

She obviously had one thing in mind when she arrived—sex. "Can we go to bed?" she said. The only bed was Tom's, which was in the basement of the storefront/gallery for the very good reason that the traffic was noisy, being right on the funny corner, and it was very dark. With Tom grumbling about being displaced from his bed (and that he was gay and had designs of his own on Frankie—not something Frankie knew until later). Paula didn't waste any time getting naked and getting to work on Frankie. Frankie's dick got so hard he could cut diamonds with it. This was a real woman. Frankie was getting an education, so this was what it was about.

Paula was from Dorchester, or "Doychesta." Even though she was from Dorchester, she didn't talk with an extreme South Boston (different from the South End) accent. Everybody else did. She would invite him to her house when the family was away and fuck his brains out. She never wore clothes. He loved watching her cook him dinner naked. She was gorgeous. Not to mention she was a lifeguard at the local pool and took acid. Wow. He was in for a real experience.

Sanctuary was in the business of helping the masses of kids who were flocking to the area to be part of the action. Harvard Square and the Cambridge Common was the destination of choice for hundreds of kids. They wanted to get away from oppressive parents trying to tell them what to do as well as police and school officials not letting them do the things they really wanted to do, like have sex, take drugs, and listen to rock and roll, like everybody else. And there was Frankie, right in the middle of it.

He never stopped to think about how he arrived; all he knew was that he was there. He never really thought about his parents, his brother, his dog. He left all that behind. He was completely here now, without a past, except for bits and pieces of a loosely fabricated one rarely inquired about. He was free, or at least not bound to anything.

Jimi was gone, then Janis was gone. Frankie had seen her perform there in Boston just a few months before then, so life was fragile. Drug overdoses. Not good. The Beatles broke up after "Let It Be."

Other than the occasional gift from someone or other, Frankie was without. He never had enough to be a problem. He didn't get it.

Paula and Frankie took trips in her light blue '64 Ford Falcon to the Cape and New Hampshire to find out-of-the-way places to throw a blanket down near a creek at the end of a dead-end road, take acid, and screw, depending on how stoned they were. There was a time she was lying on top, giving him head and him working on her other end in the hot sun. "Is everything okay?" she said.

"Yeah, good, good…"

The war in Southeast Asia still raged. The US invaded Cambodia, so student demonstrations took place in Harvard Square and the Cambridge Common, and with violent consequences, the kids were pissed and the cops were assholes. The cultural train had left the station and was roaring down the track, picking up speed, and there was Frankie.

Increasingly bolder, Frankie came into his own and used the tools he had, like being athletic, six feet, one inch, 160 pounds. He was able to take care of himself and toss out any punk causing a problem in the storefront. In the hierarchy of Sanctuary, he found himself toward the upper part of the food chain. If only they knew.

And to think he went out of his way to look as faggy as possible. Mick Jagger and Rod Stewart were troing it. It got girls. Didn't mean you couldn't kick ass like a dude; you could.

His job was to hang out with the kids, and that's what he did. He bought a Nikkormat camera from some kid (undoubtedly stolen) and began taking pictures of everybody and everything. Having a camera opened up a whole new world. Soon he was getting lessons from every photography student around.

Of course that meant taking naked pictures of Paula. She resembled the painting of Saint Bernadette in flames on the Leonard Cohen album. She had that tortured look—and was tortured. It tortured him one time when he was making love to her, and she said, "John, John! Oh, I'm sorry Frankie."

"It's okay, it's okay." John was the guy who taught her all the tricks she knew, shaved her, took pictures, and showed his friends the pictures. That John.

Frankie was front and center when the band It's a Beautiful Day played at the Cambridge Common. Photographers were given special access on stage and Frankie in the middle of it. He took full advantage, like a famous photographer.

Tom was their leader. He was the one with the vision and moxie to make Sanctuary happen. He made believers out of everyone. Staff meetings were a stage for him upon which to perform, to give his hip liturgy. And the hip part meant he was radical, antiestablishment. He was very persuasive, but he was preaching to the choir. To be radical was a way of life in Cambridge at the time.

"We have been asked to be part of the Mayor's Committee on Harvard Square," said Tom to open the Thursday staff meeting. "At the demonstrations the other day, some of the store windows were broken and other property was damaged at the Square. The mayor, the police, some of the merchants, and the local Catholic and associated churches are expressing concern about what is going on. They're forming a committee and want our input."

"Yeah, I was there and saw what happened," Frankie piped up. "Those kids are pretty pissed off. What are we supposed to do?"

"Since you seem to be the one right down in the middle of it, I think we should send you as our representative and help us figure out what to do about his," said Tom in front of everybody. These people all led sheltered lives in affluent communities (they were going to Harvard), and the staff members, who were completely clueless about what to do about the bunch of rock-throwing dissident students and drug-taking malcontents in their town, nodded their approval.

The Mayor's Committee on Harvard Square consisted of the mayor, a shiny academic named Turnbull. He was primarily concerned with his image, as were the other city council members who showed up. The Cambridge Police Department sent their cop in charge of Harvard Square (why do people who don't pronounce *r* name everything with a lot of *r*'s?)

The Cambridge Police Department sent Sargent Gallagher, a big Irish cop who'd seen about everything, he thought. Several Harvard Square merchants had terrified looks on their faces. Several local churches, of which there were many, sent their senior priests. The local underground FM station (WBCN) sent their hippest (someone decided) DJ.

"We are here today to address the problem of what to do about the demonstrations happening in Harvard Square and the property destruction taking place as a result," said Turnbull in a Kennedy-esque manner. "We must have law and order. We cannot tolerate this lawlessness" he added. "The United States government must get out of Vietnam."

"Then the demonstrations will stop," said an unappointed but angry member of the student movement in attendance of the first meeting at Cambridge City Hall.

"Throwing bricks through store windows is not a form of protest. It's vandalism," said one of the nameless, faceless city council members trying to score a few points with the contingent of merchants there. "What are the police going to do when an unruly crowd of angry protestors makes their way from the Common down Brattle to the Square and on their way to smash windows? Arrest everyone?"

"We're talking about several thousand people coming from these rallies in the common," said Father Donahue, the "somewhat sympathetic to the cause" Catholic priest.

"Many of us are against the war in Vietnam, but trashing other people's property is not going to help the cause," said another.

"How do we reach out to these kids and get across to them rioting in the streets is not the answer?" said Sargent Gallagher. He was looking directly at Frankie when he asked the question, knowing

Frankie was the only one present who had any connection with the kids doing the damage. Frankie was still kind of an empty-headed kid, so he easily shifted into a "I know but I'm not going to tell you" mode. He didn't really know anything; he was acting as though he did and was letting them think he knew something they didn't. The attention was nice, but he had better be careful; he wasn't even who he was pretending to be.

"Do you think you can talk to them and let them know we are sympathetic? Their anger is misguided. They must stop destroying property because there is a war in Southeast Asia none of us agree with," said The Sarge. Even the Police Department in Cambridge was liberal.

Frankie could see they were looking at him, having heard the counterculture slogan not to trust anyone over thirty-five, and they needed someone on the inside, a spy. Someone who would represent them in the movement of disenfranchised youth on drugs and radical students out of control, and Frankie was their boy.

He had so forgotten where he came from. He hadn't given a thought to his past; it's as if he didn't have one, at least one he wanted. Frankie was all here now and nowhere else.

The Beatles were no more, everybody hated Nixon (he was no crook), the Dead were busted for LSD possession, the Jackson 5 were big, Apollo 13 radioed "Houston, we have a problem" from space, and the Russians were setting off nuclear bombs. There was plenty to protest, and the movement was picking up steam.

After a day of steamy sex with Paula at the Seminary apartment, they were lying in the afternoon sun coming through the window. "There's something you should know, Paula," said Frankie.

"What, Frankie?" she said.

"I'm not eighteen. I'm sixteen. And I'm a runaway."

"You're what?"

"A runaway?"

"Oh, I see," she said.

He wasn't quite sure why he told her. He must have thought that she would be impressed, and it did feel good to tell somebody his secret, as much as it seemingly didn't affect him. She didn't take it too well. Maybe it wasn't the right thing to do.

It wasn't long after that Paula went to U of Mass Amherst. Frankie hitchhiked from Cambridge to visit her. He had started hanging around with some graduate students that were volunteering at Sanctuary who were studying and practicing various types of Eastern religion upon the return of Ram Dass from India. Frankie was attired in white Indian garb that Paula didn't think was too cool. "What's with the white?" It's not a style she was yet familiar with in isolated Amherst. In her dorm room were a record player and a pile of records. "Pick out some music," she said. He picked out a Jimi Hendrix record. She said, "Do you always have to be so hyper?"

"You always have to be so extreme?" Frankie went for a walk to the one store near campus, and when he came back and yelled up to have her let him in, the new "John" just waved out the window. That was it for Paula.

At a nearby dorm at the Seminary resided Ronnie White. Ronnie was a black guy who was going to ETS and volunteering at Sanctuary. He was from Delaware and a professional student. He had been through medical school, was getting his collar, and then going to Harvard Law School, of course. Ronnie had transformed himself and was the person Ram Dass depended on to coordinate the lodging and speaking engagements of the yogis and the swamis who were showing up from India at Ram Dass's invitation.

Ronnie was like a little kid. He was truly a beautiful dude and Frankie's spiritual master. He loved hanging out with Ronnie at his place. They would eat wonderful organic food and sit around and read the teachings of the great Ramana Maharshi. They would sit in front of his altar with incense and candles burning with pictures of the ones who made them high, like Saradananda, and meditate.

There was a parade of spiritual masters coming through town with big grins and the sparkle of enlightenment in their eyes; cosmic laughter was in the air, and you could hear the chanting in the chapel at ETS. They were a happy bunch.

Frankie had secured a place at Sanctuary that was of great value to the cause. There was an antiestablishment edict that was being refined and carried to its legal and not so legal end.

It involved creative counseling techniques. The technique of needing to get a person who was locked in time more stoned so then could let it go and recover and get back to being able to think, Frankie figured out. Not exactly something you could tell the powers that be, but it did work.

Frankie never went anywhere without his camera. He took pictures of everything and everybody. Someone lent him an enlarger, and he set up a darkroom in the basement of the ETS dormitory. He would get lost for hours and days there, playing with chemicals and experimenting. Time stood still in the darkroom.

It was about now that Frankie identified as being gay. It had good shock value, and he liked blowing people's minds—an act that got plenty of poontang. Girls loved hanging around with him being gay; he wasn't threatening, being gay, or seeming so.

So in a matter of a year or so, Frankie had an identity. He was a major presence at Sanctuary, a drug counselor and liaison between the establishment of Harvard Square and the young and restless crowd at the Cambridge Common, a member of the new and groovy club of followers of Eastern religion, and now not only letting everyone think he was a fag but a radical one who embraced the politics of the Gay Liberation Front. What an identity. Finally hip.

Hip was being gay, attending meetings with other radically minded young men who, yes, liked putting on makeup and dressing in drag or semidrag. Major shock value. Frankie made a great-looking boy, or girl, in drag and had many admirers. He found his way down to The Other Side, a gay bar and disco, in downtown Boston. A whole new world existed at The Other Side. It was where a new morality and sexual liberation met an underground homosexual social scene, and it rocked. Of course, all the hot bands of the day had led men who got somewhere close to semidrag themselves. Mick Jagger, Rod Stewart, Robert Plant were looking pretty gay, or at least playing with gender roles. What fun it was.

Frankie never gave a thought to what might be happening back in Sacramento. He had even forgotten about Kelly, his beloved Irish setter. It was a million miles away. He was not worried; it was as though he knew everything would be all right.

Tom proposed that some of the staff (those who were his friends, the younger members, including Frankie) get a house together and try communal living—Tom, Frankie, Marc and Mato (a young couple who grew up locally—he was Jewish and she Armenian, both very talented artists), Steve Guthrie (his father was a big shot at ETS, a kind of nice but blank fellow), and Rickie Margolin. Rickie was a Jewish kid from LA going to Harvard Medical School who volunteered until they hired him. Frankie got into Rickie's head.

Rickie's dad bought him a brand-new Volvo that they would drive up the Massachusetts coast near Manchester to a beach that had sand so clean it squeaked when you walked on it, Singing Beach. They would take acid, and Frankie would give Rickie the benefit of his vast knowledge of the universe. After a long walk on the beach, they would find a place amongst the rocks to settle in for a session of toiling with the meaning of existence. Frankie didn't toil too much; he knew the meaning and was happy to pass it along to Rickie. The ocean and far-off lighthouse lent themselves perfectly as symbols of getting here to there. Heady stuff for seventeen-year-old kids.

Just above the rocks was an abandoned castle. A real overgrown gothic stone ruin, spiral staircases climbing to the towers. It was the perfect way to go from the vastness of without to the darkness within. Maybe the boys should have started in the castle and worked their way down to a walk on the beach. Their way might have been backward, but it was a personal journey with no right way; it worked for them.

The group of staff who bought into Tom's idea of communal living got a charming six-bedroom house in Watertown near the Square. Tom was an industrious leader. There was soon furniture in the living room with a piano. There was a long table in the full-size dining room and everything one could want in a fully equipped kitchen. The best part was the basement, which was where the real fun was had. With a TV and some chairs, it was where old movies were watched late, beer and cigarettes got consumed in large quantities, and it never got cleaned. Their social experiment seemed to be a success as far as they all knew. They even inherited a wayward Golden Retriever named Rusty.

"This is Frankie, Dad," Rickie said to his father when he came to visit one day.

"So you're the one telling my boy medical school is stupid and Harvard is a fascist institution?" said his dad.

"That would be me, Pops," said Frankie.

"What right do you have telling Rick you know nothing about?" said his dad. "His mother and I have had plans for Rick to go to Harvard and become a docta for a very long time. I'm not going to let some punk ruin our plans for our son."

"I don't think Rickie sees it the same way you do, Pops," said Frankie. They were still on the front porch of the house (hadn't even gotten inside yet), and Mr. Margolin was now moving toward Frankie, who was backing down the steps. "I'm sorry he doesn't seem to agree with you about that," Frankie said while laughing at the older and smaller man, who was really steaming now. Rickie wasn't really going to drop out of school, but it was fun to fuck with his father and let him think he was.

Hazel Black was a resourceful girl—local girl, tall, beautiful, with long dirty-blond hair—who found Sanctuary, and it didn't take long to get a staff job after a brief time as a volunteer. Hazel was fascinated by Frankie and the apparent fact that he was gay and, of course, had to seduce him. She was an independent, upwardly mobile (for the time) woman with an apartment of her own in Cambridge near Sanctuary.

"If you come over tonight, I'll cook you dinner. We can listen to the Elton John record I just got," Hazel said to Frankie after a Thursday staff meeting.

"Okay," he said. "I'll be there." Frankie was knocking on the door of the upscale apartment early that night. He had on his black boots, red corduroys, skintight black leotard, silk scarf around his neck, black beret, black leather motorcycle jacket (from Tom), and two big earrings in his ears—dressed to impress. He always dressed like this. To impress…always.

"Why do you think he's gay?" she asked.

"Who?" said Frankie.

"Elton John," she said.

"I didn't know he was gay. How do you know?" he asked.

"I read it in a magazine," she said. It was as if Hazel could not comprehend that a man could want anything other than her, and Frankie was inclined to agree when their clothes came off and they hit the clean sheets of the queen bed with the large ornate walnut backboard. Hazel was all woman and made Frankie feel like a man, even though he was still a boy. He played the role and gave it to her good. Gay guys knew how to give it to a woman better. They knew what women really wanted. Hazel and Frankie became good fuck buddies.

Life at Sanctuary and the commune in Watertown was idyllic. Every night was an adventure regardless of whose night it was to cook dinner for everyone. A close bond was strengthened by weekend trips to Cape Cod, Walden Pond, and Singing Beach, on which psychedelics were taken. Innermost fears and fantasies were exposed.

But all good things come to an end, and the power play was on to take over Sanctuary by the more virtuous Peter and Dick, the two more senior members of the staff, graduate students. It turned out that they were keeping an eye on things for the more conservative members of the church overseers. They didn't say anything during the process, but after the fact brought up procedures and policies not considered acceptable, which included the creative counseling techniques, they cited the rumors that Frankie had forbidden sexual relations with a couple of young ladies (underage girls). That was actually true. But no harm had been done to anybody. The clergy should know. They had not yet been caught playing with choir boys' little PPs. It was actually to get rid of Frankie in the package deal that Tom was the target of. The takeover would actually take a while, but the groundwork had been laid to take over Tom's great idea and hard work creating Sanctuary, citing improprieties through the early days of its existence.

John was history. That John, so Paula called, and she and Frankie got together in Watertown for a quick roll in the hay. She was gorgeous as always but didn't like things out of her realm of understanding. He had lipstick on (that wouldn't come off) on their afternoon walk around Walden Pond left over from the evening before at The Other Side.

He was now a regular at the club and was making new friends. Gay friends. No one really questioned why he was sleeping with women instead of men. He was a regular on the dance floor.

Outside the club and up the street was a contingent of gay boys in semi-drag working as male prostitutes. This he found fascinating and hung around the scene. On a couple of occasions, he was picked up by creepy pervs who were patronizing the boys working in the area. He didn't make any money. He usually just bolted; it was too weird. Being a regular on the dance floor, he made contact with a black guy known as Miss Thing. Miss Thing was a woman trapped in a man's body. She was as sweet as a person can be and totally without resources of any kind, given her persona. They became inseparable although never slept together. Their primary pastime was figuring out what to wear that night at the Other Side. She did teach Frankie all the dance moves, and it wasn't long before he was a star. Frankie had to move out of his nice apartment but was able to get a more modest room (near Ronnie) for him and Miss Thing to live in while the nightlife was going on.

Through this exposure he made contact with a professional photographer who wanted to do some "female impersonation," stuff with Frankie. Frankie kind of forgot that it came with the territory. He wanted his sweet little ass. He did manage to get some good pictures before he denied the guy.

It didn't take long for Hazel to seduce Tom, and they carried on a pretty full-time thing, even though Tom was gay, or half gay, bi.

Frankie was hanging out at Judy Reed's house, a beautiful old place heading out of Harvard Square. She was older (maybe thirty), had an architect husband (never before seen), and had a staff job at Sanctuary.

After the first bottle of wine, Judy asked, "What about your parents?"

"San Francisco," he replied.

"What does your father do for a living?"

"He's an engineer," he said.

"How did you end up here in Cambridge?" she asked.

That was something no one had asked him before. He hadn't prepared himself for that one because, of course, everybody wanted to go to California, not come from California to butt-ass cold New England from where it was happening. "Ahh, well, Judy, to be honest with you, I'm really seventeen and a runaway," he said. He wasn't quite sure why he told her, but other than Paula, she was the only person he had given away the secret to. Maybe it just felt good to tell someone. Maybe it was the wine or that it felt good to share his secret, but the cat was out of the bag. His time with Sanctuary was coming to an end; it was time for a change.

"You promise not to tell anyone, Judy?" he asked a little too late.

"Of course, I won't tell anyone," she said. She promptly called Tom and told him the news—not that it mattered anyway since the coup was underway and that there would be a successful takeover. It was good gossip.

"I was wondering why you were so anxious to show me your ID when I first met you," said Tom when he pulled up to the corner (as if a trick. Did he know this corner?) in his car at the meat rack across from the Other Side, where Frankie was acting like a sweet young white boy out to suck some cock for money.

"So now you know, it's true," said Frankie.

"I somehow knew that you could not have done all the things you claim to have done," he said rather admiringly. Tom was actually impressed that the kid pulled off being two years older than he was. The kid fooled everyone, and they had over a year to get to know him. "What about your parents?" he asked.

"I'm heading back to California sometime soon," he said. "They won't be seeing me for a while, though," said Frankie, not wanting to reveal more than he already had. He was, after all, a runaway.

He batted his false eyelashes, dying to get back inside the club, and said, "I'm having too much fun to worry about that right now. See ya, Tom." He went back into the hot, sweaty club with music pounding and bodies pulsating, found Miss Thing, and headed onto the crowded dance floor.

It was the spring of 1970. Charles Manson was on trial for the Tate Bianca murders, there were race riots in Georgia, Nixon signed a bill lowering the voting age to eighteen, the Beatles broke up (this time for sure) then released "Let It Be," war in Vietnam raged on, and antiwar protests grew. Historic days, almost as profound as the few years that proceeded that year. It's not like he was up on politics, only how it affected him.

He was walking up Mass Avenue near Central Square one day coming from a Gay Liberation Front meeting (its main focus was to talk about who was gay and to listen to T Rex. Mark Bolan was gay). "Hey, Frankie, what's going on?"

"Going to the square. What's up?"

"Hey, you wanna smoke some opium?" this kid whom he barely knew from Sanctuary said. He was impressed. He hadn't actually smoked opium before. "Yeah, I guess." They walked up the street and found a parking lot off the street to catch a buzz on what was supposedly opium. A police car spotted them and moved in to see what these long-haired fellows were up to. "I'm a member of the Mayor's Committee on Harvard Square. I'm giving this guy some counseling," said Frankie with conviction.

"Yeah, sure you are. What do you have there?" said the cop.

"Nothing," said the kid with the O.

"Hey, Charlie, you seen this b'fore?" the cop asked his partner, holding up the pipe and a little ball of O that he had taken out of the guy's pocket.

"I think that's opium, you know, like heroin," said the partner. "Turn around, put your hands behind your back." They were arrested and taken to Central Square station.

"Hey, I was trying to help this kid out. I'm giving him counseling," said Frankie. "I'm on the Mayor's Committee on Harvard Square. Ask Sergeant Gallagher!" Frankie said to the cop who was trying to get what they were doing there and why.

"How do you know Sergeant Gallagher?" asked the cop.

"I told you, I'm on the Mayor's Committee on Harvard Square, so is Sergeant Gallagher. Go ask him," Frankie said.

A couple of hours passed and finally the good sergeant came in and was walking toward the holding cell flanked by the two curious cops wanting to see if and how was it that the good sergeant was on a first-name basis with this freak they busted red-handed trying to smoke opium, a hard drug. "Frankie, what're ya doing here? Get him outta thea," he said to the arresting cop.

"I was just trying to work with this kid, Sarge," Frankie said impishly.

"I know you were, Frankie, and it's a good thing ya doing out thea." It was good to have a little clout, even if you weren't who you were pretending to be.

At the Other Side, Frankie met a bull dyke (lesbian) named Crystal. Crystal was a clone of the girl who shadowed Andy Warhol, who was pretty hot at the time.

Everyone "cool" ran down to the chic salons on Marlboro Street in Boston to get a shag haircut. A shag was the first cut to clean up long hair—short on top, long on the sides stylin'. Crystal had the look of a model, with curly blond hair cut into a shag. So Frankie, who had a shag, of course, and Crystal connected and hung out together.

Just as it got wanted attention for a guy to be gay, it also got attention for a girl to be gay too, and that's the kind of bull dyke Crystal was. She wore cowboy shirts and put on a tough persona, but she really wanted to fuck the shit out of Frankie as well. Late one night at Frankie's Seminary studio apartment at ETS, they found themselves in bed. Frankie lay on his back, and Crystal climbed on him and slipped her very wet pussy around his very stiff cock. They fucked like maniacs and came in a chorus of screams. They weren't very gay now.

It was time to go back to California. His eighteenth birthday was coming up. He still had a year. Lucky for Frankie and Miss Thing, Crystal wanted to drive to LA that summer in the new Volvo station wagon that her rich parents (probably U of Mass Amherst alumni) bought her. Frankie packed a couple hundred pounds of crap he collected (books stolen from the basement of ETS) in the back of that wagon. They stopped at her parents' beautiful house in western Mass (mainly to raid the food supply for the trip). Neither Frankie nor Miss Thing had any money, so the entire trip would be financed by Crystal.

When they got to Chicago, they were driving around down-town looking for a gay bar and came across a guy walking his dog in a warehouse area. "Do you know where the Paradise Club is?" asked Crystal.

"That's all the way on the other side of town," said the guy. "You guys need directions? I live right here. Come on in," he said. The three were quite a sight, and the invitation suggested he really just wanted to get a better look at them. That was cool; they liked the attention.

"You live here?" asked Frankie, pointing to a warehouse.

"Yeah, come on in," he said.

The guy was a professional photographer and had converted a large warehouse space into a studio and a very nice luxury studio/loft/gallery space. It was a large structure in the middle of the space. The structure had a kitchen and an outrageous bath and sauna. On top was a large luxurious bed. It was very inviting and clearly a playboy pad. That's right, *Playboy*—wasn't that from Chicago?

"My name is Daniel. Who are you? You're looking for a gay bar? Not around here, but there are a couple over on the East Side. You sure you got the right city?"

"I'm Frankie," he said, looking rather wide-eyed. "Crystal and Wes. We call her Miss Thing," he added, as the two stepped up, smiling.

"Can we use your bathroom?" asked Crystal with some urgency.

"Yeah, of course, it's right there." He pointed.

"I'm a photographer too," said Frankie.

"What are you doing in this part of Chicago? If you don't mind my asking," said Daniel.

"Someone in Boston told us to check out the Paradise Club, so we just pulled off the freeway," said Frankie.

"I can give you directions if you like. It's a long way from here. You can stay here tonight if you like and go there tomorrow," said Daniel.

"That would be great, thanks," said Frankie. He yelled to the two in the bathroom, "He says we can stay here tonight!"

"Great," said Crystal. "Wow, you oughta see the bathroom," she added.

They were tired, and Daniel situated them for the night. The three of them watched as a couple of different hot broads paid a visit to Daniel's upstairs bed. It was obvious that this guy was doing something very special that these women liked very much, and the phone was ringing off the hook. Daniel was a very virile fellow.

The next day Daniel took Frankie on a shoot to show the kid how a real photographer worked. He set up a ladder on the median in the middle of Lake Shore Drive after negotiating swiftly through moving traffic upon which to stand to take pictures of a building for a corporate client. He earned his money that day.

Rested, the trio thanked Daniel for his hospitality and hopped into the Volvo and hit the road. It wasn't like they had any drugs to make the trip more interesting or radio stations playing any music they liked. The Midwest was kind of a bore. They wouldn't know even if they had a clue. Colorado was ahead, and that meant cowboy shirts that Crystal so desired, Frankie too. They got to a cowboy shirt town, and Crystal shopped. She bought Frankie one and several for herself. Next stop, San Francisco.

They would be coming to the Sierras soon, and being midsummer, Frankie knew there was a good chance that his family (Arnie, Joni, Dana, Jason, his younger brothers) would be on vacation at their favorite spot at an alpine lake named Union Valley Reservoir, where they would fish and ski from their ski boat and have a good time. Frankie had a little convincing to do but was successful in talking Crystal into driving out of the way to the parking lot where the car and boat trailer would be parked, and there they were. It was a long hike to the campsite down a fire road, but Frankie had done it many times in previous years.

The campsite was in an inlet of the lake, which on one side had perfect rock off which to dive into the clear lake water. He observed his brother diving off the rock into the water on the hot summer day from behind a tree up on the other side where the tree line began. He quietly tried to get his brother's attention but couldn't. It was better that he didn't because his stupid brother would have ratted him out. He snuck back along the tree line, to the fire road, and to the parking lot. Crystal and Miss Thing weren't exactly pissed but getting bored with the quiet and the natural beauty and wanted to get going. But not until Frankie wrote them a letter. It said:

Dear Dad and Joni,

I'm glad to see you're doing well. I'm fine. I bet you're wondering when or if you were ever going to hear from me again. I have been traveling. As you know, I will not be eighteen for almost another year, so you will not be seeing me until then. I want to let you know I love you and not to worry. I'll be fine.

Love, Frankie

When the family got back to the car and read the note, they freaked. They couldn't believe Frankie happened to have come all the way up there when they were there and left such a note. They hadn't forgotten about him but had obviously moved on with their lives. Joni cried. They all knew damn well why the kid beat it. They were the ones who equipped him with the survival skills and then tried to hold him down. His note didn't include that he had left their clutches an empty-headed kid and returned a drug counselor and counselor of runaways, an official member of the Mayor's Committee on Harvard Square, a photographer, a student of Eastern religion, and gay (or so it seemed).

Gaining independence from what was an oppressive environment was by all accounts a success story. He gained independence as a result of mainly Arnie forcing down his throat what a dog-eat-dog world it was out there. Arnie's version of the world was much more sinister than the one Frankie found. In fact, it all seemed to come pretty easy in a time of the new utopian vision that the counter culture had. "Tune in, turn on, drop out!" was pretty easy to achieve. There would be much more of that to come.

It was the plan for Crystal to go to LA where she had a hot and heavy rendezvous with someone of the same sex. She was glad the journey was over and glad to be done with supporting these two, as wonderfully entertaining as they were.

When they got to Berkeley, Frankie got in touch with Dak, who, it turned out, lived in and managed an old rundown apartment building on California Street off of University Avenue. Conveniently there was room for Frankie and Miss Thing in the building.

"Time to get a job, Frankie," said Dak. "You're a fashion hound. Get a job in a clothing store," he said.

"How come I didn't hear from you in Boston? What about those letters to Patrice?"

"I didn't forward them. With Neptune around, it was just too risky," said Dak. Frankie didn't like that answer because he got the feeling Dak was interfering in a relationship with a girl—something Dak didn't like even though there was nothing other than friendship between them. Dak had a live-in golden boy. Bobby was a beautiful local boy who never shaved and had the most wonderful curly blond beard ever seen. There was no good reason to go to that extent to protect him when he was all the way back east in Boston, at least that what was Frankie figured.

He put on his fanciest duds and hit the pavement. Being freaky was an asset for a clothing or shoe store of the time to send the message that the business was hip and should be patronized by young people. His first job was at a shoe store on Polk Street, which didn't last. He then got work on The Ave at a clothing store that was popular and had hip attire, Piccadilly. It was here that Frankie was introduced to cocaine. A hardened-looking guy with curly black hair came in one day and was looking at clothing, eyeing Frankie, trying to assess if he was cool enough to ask, "Wanna do some coke?"

He was looking for a safe place to shoot up and wanted to go into the back. "My name is Chaz, from New York. What's yer name?" he asked.

"I'm Frankie," he said. Chaz sat down in the rear of the store storage room, took out a spoon, set it on a box, reached into his pocket, and pulled out a folded-up piece of magazine paper, unfolded it, scooped out a small amount of white powder contained within, and put it in the spoon. "Got water?" he said.

"Yeah, just a minute." He went and got a cup of water. Chaz took out a syringe and drew some water into it then squirted the water into the spoon and mixed it up. "Got a cigarette?" Frankie gave him a cigarette. Chaz took the filter off, took a ball of cotton, and dropped it into the spoon. He drew the clear mixture into the syringe through the cotton ball in the spoon, held it up, squeezed the plunger until the air was out, and set it down. He took off his belt, rolled up his sleeve, and put the belt around his upper arm. The inner part of his arm at the elbow was a small scab that he flicked off, and out of a small hole blood began to ooze. "Trap door," he said. He dropped the needle into the hole, drew the plunger out until blood came into the syringe, took the belt off, and depressed the plunger. "Aaaaaaaooooooohhh yeah," said Chaz. He laid back with eyes closed and mouth open. "Oh, that's nice," he said.

That was when the store door ringer began ringing and grabbed Frankie's attention. In came some customers, right when Frankie was about to learn to fly. Out walked Chaz with a crazed look on his face, never to be seen again. Frankie's time would come for that first buzz, but not today.

Miss Thing discovered The Big Basket on Kearny just off Broadway in the City. The Big Basket was a grand gay dance club that rocked until 6:00 a.m. It was an all-night affair with dancing, cock sucking, and certainly butt fucking happening in the bathroom and in the dark booths in the corners of the club. She found someone to love and was gone from Frankie's life, never to be heard from again.

The apartment building was a dive, even though it was kind of fun, and Dak needed money for the place, so Frankie went to the Free Church, which was now on Blake and Milvia to see what Ray was up to. He was hanging around what was now a bona fide small church with lots of room to hang out, smoke cigarettes, drink coffee, and play chess.

"Hey, Ray, how's it going?" asked Frankie when he saw Ray, who was wearing a collar under the blond beard and long hair.

"Frankie!"

"You look like a different person, you look great!"

"Where have you been?" he said.

"Well, it's a long story. I've been in Boston, and I'm back. Looking for a place to stay. Know of anything?"

"I got tons of space. Wait until you see this place," said Ray.

He had a huge turn-of-the-century Tudor mansion in downtown Oakland (long since torn down) on Twelfth and Grove Streets. It must have been at least eight thousand if not ten thousand square feet. It was three stories, with six full-size suites with enormous rooms. It was old and run-down, and he was supposedly doing some work on it for the realtor he knew while he lived in it.

He and a Chinese guy were more like squatting in the place along with some wacky frizzed-out blonde broad and her Mexican boyfriend. The place was so grand it had its own theater next door. Built in the days of the opulence and decadence of the very upper class, it lent itself to the current abuse to that of the days of old. The current occupants gathered in tribute to that, without a clue of what it meant.

Ray gave Frankie his own suite in which to squat. He was pretty good and creating illusions and getting people to believe they were true. Ray had a good and generous heart and knew the real Frankie. So Frankie never thought for a minute he could pull the wool over Ray's eyes. He didn't need to; the digs were most satisfactory.

The wacky frizzed-out blonde with the Mexican boyfriend, Elaine, had a suite in another part of the house, and she said to him, "I've never met a guy with two earrings before. That's outta sight." This freaky hippie chick thought Frankie was "outta sight." He had arrived.

The Chinese guy was in possession of the theater and had it full of antiquities, furniture, and lots of collectables. A lot of junk too. Frankie was quick to raid the mountain of shit to furnish his new apartment. Nobody was going to miss a few items from the huge pile of relics, he thought. He helped himself to the goods.

Frankie was walking down The Ave to work one day, wearing white potato toe shoes, tight wide wale, orange bell-bottomed corduroy pants, tight Danskin leotard top, white women's jacket (waist high) from the '30s with padded shoulders (never before worn due to the fact it was so large for a woman, so it fit perfectly), and two good-sized earrings bouncing from under his shag haircut. He came face-to-face with Kim.

Kim had on snakeskin platform boots (from Rainbow Cobbler in the City, very expensive), doeskin pants with unfinished edges, slightly belled top with fur collar (custom made at North Beach Leather, very expensive), Navajo silver turquoise bracelets and neck chain, shag haircut, and hand-carved cane.

They walked directly up to one another, both thinking, *Who is this?* "How's it going?" said Frankie, and he stuck out his hand.

"Very good, and you?" said Kim.

They got to Piccadilly, and Frankie said, "I work here." "Let's get together some time."

"Sounds good. I'll come by later. Maybe dinner tonight," said Kim.

"Sounds good." Koreans only eat Korean food, so the obvious choice for dinner was the Korean restaurant on Telegraph. The food is the spiciest of any in the world, not to mention served boiling. Kim slurped the whole bowl down before Frankie could sip a spoonful, and he was already sweating from the kimchi and pickled radish marinated in red pepper appetizer. Frankie learned right off the bat this Korean could do something he could not. The next day it felt like burning embers came out of his ass when he took a shit.

"You said you were going to Cal. What's your major?" asked Frankie later the next day.

"I'm not really going right now," said Kim. "I dropped out and went traveling."

"Where did you go?" asked Frankie.

"Cambridge Mass," he said.

"Really, when were you there?" asked Frankie.

"About a year ago, during the riots in Harvard Square," he said. "I was thinking of going to Harvard, but hanging out and getting high is more fun. That's what I've been doing since then."

"Wow, that's amazing. I was in Cambridge then, far out," said Frankie. "If you were hanging out in the Common, I bet I have a picture of you."

"I was always at the Common. I used to wear overalls then," he said, then he changed his fashion statement quite a bit. "You do coke?" he asked.

"Yeah," said Frankie, not being truthful.

"Let's go get some," he said. They walked down Durant Avenue to Ellsworth and went into the large Victorian in the middle of the block (west side) called the Green House. It had the distinct look of being inhabited by hippies. A guy with long blond hair answered the door and said, "Hey, Kim, how ya doin'?"

"This is Frankie," said Kim, and the guy shook his hand.

"How ya doin'?" said John.

"Got any coke?" asked Kim.

"Tracy just left. She should be back in about an hour or so," he said.

John was the owner of the house, and they walked upstairs to the main parlor to wait for Tracy. Tracy walked in the room with very beady eyes. She was a frizzed-out-looking little chick who lived in the dump behind the Green House. "Tracy, got a gram?" asked Kim.

"Yeah, let me take care of John first," said Tracy.

"Can I get a needle?" asked Kim of John.

"Okay," he said and gave him a new (in the package) hypodermic needle for injecting insulin. John was diabetic. Kim performed the routine he saw happen in the back room at Piccadilly. Kim put the tie around his arm, gritting his teeth, holding the end of the tie, veins bulging; found one; stuck in the needle; got blood, undid the tie; and injected the mixture. He put a cotton on the spot, closed his arm, laid back on the bed with eyes closed, and said, "Oh, that's nice. What a feeling. Yyyyyeeeeeaaaaaahhhhhhh!"

Tracy was an expert and began cleaning the needle and preparing to give herself a shot. When she pulled her sleeve up, Frankie could see by the tracks on her arm she was indeed an expert. She gave herself a shot without fanfare and began cleaning the needle. "Make one up for Frankie," said Kim.

"Is this your first time?" asked Tracy, who seemed unfazed by the shot of coke she had just injected.

"Yeah," said Frankie. "Make sure you don't miss. You'll get an abscess. Be sure to release the tie when you hit the vein. Get blood in the syringe," she said.

He was ready. He was surprised at how sharp it was. Blood filled the syringe. He released the tie and injected the coke into his arm.

The lights in the room began ringing; the walls were vibrating. He got a chemical taste in his mouth and a warm vibration came over him. He'd never felt anything like that before. He could only say, "Oh my god, this is incredible." It was angel trumpets and devil trombones. He would never again get the thrill of his first shot because it was now behind him.

Now he just wanted more to continue the feeling, but it was John's turn, and the attention was on the others before him who had the ways and means to have more.

Frankie was smoking a cigarette one day in front of Piccadilly, and coming down The Ave was a tan beauty with long brown hair, a regal Roman lookalike with horse-like features (good horse-like features—broad nose, high cheekbones), perfect round breasts bouncing unsupported underneath a sheer see-through light-blue genie-looking outfit, with bells jingling and jewelry jangling. She was barefoot.

"Hey, where are you going?" said Frankie.

"Oh, just walking around," she said.

"What's your name?" he asked.

"Bobby," she said. "What's yours?"

"Frankie. Want to come over and hang out at my place later?" he asked.

"Sure, sounds good. Where do you live?" asked she.

"Oakland, not far," he said. Frankie was smitten with the brown-haired, brown-eyed beauty as they sat on the bus going down Telegraph. "Do you work?" he asked.

"I work at the Garden of Earthly Delights on Broadway in the City," she said. She was a stripper at a nudie bar, and he didn't really know what that was and didn't care. It was clear by the time they got to their stop she was going to fuck Frankie's brains out. They were young and strong and horny as hell and fucked like a couple of ban-shees until their strength was gone.

"Where do you live?" he asked.

"I'm staying with my girlfriend here in Berkeley," she said.

"Wanna move in here?" he said.

"Yeah, right now. Fuck me some more." Young, hot, and sweaty sex was what life was about.

Rod Stewart was hot, and Frankie cut his hair like his. Led Zeppelin was a monster band whom they loved. Politics was less important even though the United States was still in Vietnam. The SDS was in full swing, and they professed armed struggle against the military industrial complex with the demonic figurehead Richard Nixon who was universally hated by all. The cultural revolution was slowly but surely becoming more mainstream. Everybody and his brother now had long hair, and everyone else was at least showing signs of acceptance to the shift in social attitude. What at one time had good shock value was now commonplace. Wearing fancy clothes and cutting his hair now made Frankie "pseudo hip." There was a purist element who now passed judgment on everyone else, and nothing rose to their standards of absolute rejection of everything normal in American society. One could not be radical enough to rise to heights now unattainable for your average hippie. You had to be more radical than everybody else, they said, in Berkeley, ground zero.

When Bobby wasn't working during the day, she would lay out naked on the roof of the mansion. Elaine's Mexican boyfriend would look out their bedroom window above and get all horny, she told Frankie. She did indeed have a smoking brown body that could entice men to get excited. She'd lay there with her legs spread and a big smile on her face. Frankie was lucky to be getting such good poontang.

The real fun was had when The Who or Led Zeppelin came to town. They would get all dolled up like they were the rock stars and hit the town. The two attracted a lot of attention and met up with similarly minded young people who wanted to hang out too.

When he wasn't stepping out with Bobby, he was hanging out with Kim and their new friend Clayton. Clayton was a black guy who came into Piccadilly and bought a crazy mod orange overalls with a purple top. He was a colorful addition to fashion groundbreaking Kim and Frankie. They would have made a perfect band, but they really only walked all over Berkeley and talked and looked the part.

Clayton, it turned out, was a thief. He would wander into office buildings and somehow find people's wallets and purses and somehow lift them. It was pretty impressive to see the crisp hundred-dollar bills, and he was very generous with them.

These relationships were totally free and without possession. Everyone was always free to do whatever they wanted whenever they wanted. Frankie knew that Bobby made her tips at the Garden of Earthly Delights by guys rolling up dollars bills and sticking them up her pussy. It was a job, a very intimate job.

Frankie took advantage of the freedom himself and had another friend named New York Dan. Dan was coming down The Ave one day and saw Frankie standing in front of the clothing store. He was interested in meeting Frankie for his seemingly heterosexual demeanor. He knew the clothes and the earrings were not to attract men but women. He wanted to know this kid because he was a magnet for chicks, and Dan wanted chicks.

Dan was tall and manly with long brown hair and a mustache. He was very good-looking in a conventional way, with a pronounced jaw and strong forehead. He wore a black velvet cape and Sir Walter Raleigh boots. He looked as though he stepped out of a *Three Musketeers* movie, dashing. "New York Dan," he said as he stuck out his hand to the much younger and boyish-looking Frankie.

"Frankie," he said and shook his hand.

"I bet you snag plenty of pussy hanging out here…kind a like fishing, huh," said Dan.

"No doubt. There are some pretty college girls walking up and down the street." He just gave a smile without giving a rundown on how many exactly. He was not one to kiss and tell—too cool.

"So you work here huh?" he asked.

"Yeah."

"Let's see what ya got," he said and went in. He wandered around and said, "Nice. I know a beauty who's looking for some fun tonight. Wanna come?"

"Sure, why not? Where?"

"Here, in Berkeley. I have a car," said Dan.

Dan and Frankie drove to a house on Alcatraz, where they entered the living room. Seeing the dining room, kitchen, and adjoining rooms looked like it probably looked eighty years ago.

Out of the kitchen came bounding a voluptuous hippie chick with a full-length sheer dress exposing her huge tits bouncing around liberally with all the other parts.

"Oh, Dan, you're here," she said and ran up and put her arms around him and kissed him. "Who's this?" she said, turning to look at Frankie."

"Frankie is here for the same thing I am," said Dan.

"Oh, the more the merrier," she said. Carmen was a full-sized woman with a full bush, probably of Irish descent, with rosy cheeks and dirty blond hair, and she was very bouncy. She liked showing off her large breasts. "Come on, baby," she said, and Dan and she slammed the door to the bedroom. The roar of passion came out through the door in the form of screams and moans for about ten minutes. "Your turn," he said after he came out of the bedroom. "She's waiting for you."

Frankie got up from the chair he was sitting in and walked into the dark bedroom of the dingy dwelling. He walked in to see the hefty woman lying on her back with her legs spread as much as she could. With a blissful look on her face, she said, "You're cute, honey. Come give it to me."

Frankie could not be rude and not want some five fleshy bumps (it was good and dark) lying there. "Am I hurting you?"

"No, no, no, don't stop, don't stop!" she shouted. He pounded away on the roomy wet hole until she wound up yelping and moaning to a final place where the journey ended in a silent leap with the unknown, a gasp of air in free fall of climax.

Frankie was glad that was over as he unclamped her hands from around him. "Oh, baby, that was soooooo good," she said as he got off the bed.

"Yeah, it was great," he said as he buttoned up and slipped out of the room. They were out the door before she came out of the bedroom.

Frankie and Dan would share a rich pastime of driving around spotting chicks walking down the street. Dan would convince the girl to take them home, and it was pretty obvious what he wanted—for her to fuck their brains out. Frankie never really wanted it that bad, which, of course, made him much more desirable. The image of a girl looking over Dan's shoulder while he was humping away and she wanting Frankie while she was getting basically raped by Dan was something he saw more than once. It wasn't pretty. It was taking full advantage of the "free love, peace, no war" ethic they all as obedient little Berkeley children of the revolution were required to do to prove their independence from the mainstream American establishment, even if it didn't feel right. Frankie would learn from Dan the means by which a real hustler got his way, without working too hard, in a world where the fruit was ripe for plucking from the tree.

With an identity that could pop out from behind a tree and say "Boo!" the seventeen-year-old runaway knew he could not live by poontang alone; there was more to life, like getting high.

He found Kim at Tracy's behind the Green House. "Hey, what's happening, Kim?" he asked as Kim came out from Tracy's bedroom. There was no sex involved; everybody was much too fucked up to think about sex, and Tracy was not fuckable anyway. Stepping over all the crap that was on the floor because there was nowhere else to put it, Kim wasn't looking too healthy. It was obvious they were shooting coke. "You want to shoot some coke?" he asked.

"Yeah, sure," said Frankie. *I want to get all fucked up and look like you.* He really didn't know much about Kim. He knew he was from a rich Korean family. Grandpa was a distiller of whiskey, or whatever they called it in Korea, and made a fortune. In one of their walks around Berkeley, he heard the story of how the limousine would deliver his hot soup lunch while the other kids had to eat theirs cold. Made him feel guilty, he said. UC Berkeley or Harvard, take your pick. Mother was sending him money that he was financing a never-ending binge for him and his lowly friends hanging on tightly for the free ride. It brought acceptance and the hangers-on showed their appreciation by holding their spoons out for another hit. Frankie got his, and the filthy walls buzzed and the hazy sun shone through the tattered curtains of the aluminum-framed cheap window.

The brand of enlightenment was not dependent on that high level of living you would think necessary in order to step away from and get that bliss. It was a minute of bliss in a pile of garbage—and another and another and another. They were real zombies now.

After several days of shooting coke, Kim finally stood up and made clear to everyone that he was overamping. "Call an ambulance!" said Tracy as she stood up and put her hands on top of his to keep him from raising them, but she was unsuccessful. "Put something in his mouth!" she said. "So not to let him swallow his tongue." John lowered him to his back and pressed his fingers between his upper and lower teeth to force open his mouth. "Don't put your fingers in his mouth. Here, put this on his tongue," said Tracy as she handed him a tongue depressor conveniently placed within reach of the inevitable event. They had been through this before.

The ambulance came and took Kim to Alta Bates a few blocks away. Frankie was pretty fucked up but ran to the emergency room where Kim had been taken to give him any comfort and support he could. Kim was now revived and giving the staff of the hospital a fit by standing on the gurney used to wheel him into the trauma room so they could get what was going on with this bizarrely dressed Korean kid. He wouldn't cooperate at all and gave Frankie a very dirty look when he said, "Kim, Kim, they're trying to help you." Frankie realized immediately that Kim was fine and pissed off because he spoke his name to the authoritarian hospital staff trying to help him (everybody from Korea's name was Kim.) He was an illegal alien from Korea whose visa had expired and was now a criminal. Screw the fact he was trying to swallow his tongue and had a seizure from shooting too much coke less than an hour before that.

They gave up. Kim just wanted to get the fuck out of there, and they let him go. He made his way back to his friend Pallop's house (a school friend who lived on Dwight near the Green House) and lay shivering under a blanket safe and sound away from the powers that be with ambulances and hospitals of the evil empire endangering his freedom from doing the things he wanted to do. Those powers never had a clue and could have cared less who he was or where he was from; they were just trying to help him from what he had done to himself. It was a miracle he survived himself.

Amid the excitement, Frankie decided to take up residence near the action in the basement of the Green House. Bobby hadn't been seen in a while—not that Frankie was around. Moving to the eye of the storm seemed like the logical thing to do. He didn't know any logic, but he didn't want to miss anything.

Frankie borrowed Tracy's 1950 Chevy Suburban truck to move the furniture he had helped himself to (stole) from the Chinese guy at Ray's place at night. But he figured out that Frankie was the guy who stole his treasures and was ready to pounce the night Frankie showed up with the truck to move all the ill-gotten goods.

As he was moving the stuff, the very pissed-off and very muscular Chinaman came charging out of the darkness of the hallway outside his place and tackled Frankie with a vengeance he had not expected. Though thin and faggy, Frankie was a stud and knew the extent of his strength, which was formidable. He was tough, and he knew it, but this Chinaman was now getting the best of him; it was time to turn on the fury. He rose to the occasion and beat the guy back enough to turn the tide and deliver the message, not through aggression but self-defense, that the attack would not go the Chinaman's way, even though he was the one being ripped off. Frankie got the goods in the truck and got the hell out of there.

He would be uninvited by John, whose house it was, who did not know that Frankie moved into the basement of the Green House with all his newly pilfered goods. An antique couch, classic hand-carved chest of drawers, a large round mirror, antique rug, and lighting just sitting there, not used by anybody. John would be unhappy about it later when he found out about it. For now, what he didn't know didn't hurt him.

It would be a short-lived situation. Kim decided to stop shooting coke and wanted to get an apartment in the City and wanted Frankie to maybe live with him, with his cool new furnishings.

They got a place on Hermann Street across from the Mint in a very fancy elaborately appointed Victorian. Through Dan's connections, Frankie got a job doing construction work at a new club in North Beach called North Beach Revival.

Here Frankie would learn about construction and do the honest work of painting and decorating. He already had a head start doing carpentry due to the fact his Uncle Marv was a carpenter and he decided early on he wanted to do that too when he helped him build cabinets for Arnie's garage. Scott was a foreman of the job and representative for the owner's interest in creating the hip new nightclub, music venue, and three-star restaurant. The owners were hip businessmen Bill and Mike, who owned North Beach Leathers on Vallejo Street next to the Trieste Cafe on the corner of Grant Avenue. Their partners were Voss and Emile, Italian mobsters. Voss was the owner of the On Broadway, the original home of Carol Doda—the silicone-boobed (paid for by Voss) goddess and main attraction in North Beach. He actually started with The Off Broadway on Kearny, which became The North Beach Revival. Emile was the godfather, maître d' of New Joe's (San Francisco's original Original Joe's) next to Enrico's. They owned everybody and everything in North Beach, including the cops. For gangsters, they were nice guys, if you were on their side.

The painting and decorating came in handy in the new apartment. Frankie was able to get his hands on some of the choice colors of paint used in the club and some dishware and art Dan was pushing to get Scott to buy for the club. Frankie had some sticky fingers when it came to nice things and didn't realize what thin ice he was treading on stealing from gangsters and not to mention Dan, who would have kicked his ass.

The apartment living-room walls got painted designer dark red, the coved ceiling flat black, and the picture molding, baseboard, mantel silver, with an orange silk Indian tapestry (one he got from Dak, who gave him his strong sense of hip decor) hanging from the ceiling with bright lighting softened and creating orange light. Psychedelic but tasteful. Then, of course, it was furnished with the fancy Victorian furniture. The boys were living in style. It was a good thing Kim had some dough and Frankie had the where-with-all and artistic touch to create the ultimate party pad for the two to get high in and stay high in. Kim took the credit even though he didn't do anything to bring it to reality except pay the bills.

Frankie was walking past The Condor on the corner of Broadway and Columbus, and a guy near the front door said, "Spare change?" Frankie gave the guy a quarter and headed up Grant Avenue. Apparently the barker at The Condor mistakenly fingered Frankie to a couple of cops in a car and, wrong or right, seized the opportunity to pull into the alley where the famous Saloon is located, grab Frankie, and throw him in the back of the squad car.

Frankie had on his usual costume of half women's clothes and half mod attire—velvet pants, potato toed shoes (now silver), earrings, long hair. It was an outfit that did not appeal to cops. "You cocksucking, motherfucking cops!" he screamed and kicked the living shit out of the inside of the cop car. "I didn't do anything, you fucking assholes!" he screamed.

The barker arrived on the scene and said, "No, this isn't the guy," but it was too late. He had already pissed off the cops, so it really didn't matter what he had done. Give the panhandler a quarter—he was going to jail for loitering. They took him to jail and rather than plead guilty and be released, Frankie decided to plead not guilty. The lineup of drunks and derelicts going through the formality of pleading guilty to a minor charge which got dismissed all turned to look at Frankie as well as everybody in the courtroom. For that, he would have to come back for trial. Good thing nobody noticed he might not be eighteen and have his parents' permission to be there. Frankie would get another lesson in how corrupt and dishonest cops, judges, and the entire criminal justice system was and how little it had to do with justice.

Other than that, Frankie was a stand-up guy. He did still have an affinity for gay bars.

He hung around a gay bar on Grant Avenue named The Capri and a dyke bar on upper Broadway and Stockton (right by the tunnel) called The Wild Side West, frequented by Janis Joplin when she was in town. It was a very old Barbary Coast saloon with all kinds of shit hanging off the ceiling (ceilings built in that era were at least twelve feet high, or higher). It was pool tables dominated with authority by truck-driving butchy-butch dykes who would kick your teeth in if you looked at them wrong.

Here he ran into Theda and Rainbow. Theda and Rainbow, formerly members of the Cockettes, splintered off into a more extreme (if there was such a thing) form of gay guerrilla theater known as The Angels of Light. Rainbow, of American Indian descent, was like Miss Thing, a woman trapped in a man's body. She was always in full drag, wearing tight glittery 1920s CanCan dresses and jewelry to die for. She would not be mistaken for a man.

Theda was of common "Cockette" stock—overweight, beard encrusted in glitter, feathers shooting out, gobs of jewelry, laughing. Frankie knew how to get in with freaks like this. He wanted to be one too. He wore women's clothes; they warmed up to the pretty boy.

"Hey, honey, where did you get those shoes?" Theda asked Frankie.

"In Boston, they're granny shoes," said Frankie.

"Nice. I'm Theda. This is Rainbow."

"Hi," said Frankie.

"What's yer name, honey?"

"Frankie. What do you do?" asked Frankie.

"We used to be in The Cockettes but now have a group of our own, The Angels of Light. We're always looking for talent. You look talented," said Rainbow.

"I can do anything. What kind of talent are you talking about?"

They laughed knowingly with dirty minds active with well-cultivated fantasies. "Singing, dancing, acting, sucking cock," they said amid the laughter. Frankie was not about to reveal his secret of acting gay and not being gay, so at least he could act.

Frankie would now dedicate his time, when he wasn't working construction at North Beach Revival, to hanging out with Theda and Rainbow. That meant getting into full drag and going to parties around town, attending midnight shows at the Palace Theater in Washington Square after the Chinese movies ran and just causing a commotion wherever they went. The shows at the Palace Theater after midnight were phenomenal.

Performances by The Cockettes, The Angels of Light, Sylvester (at one time a member of the Cockettes went on to bigger and better things, even a record contract), Carol Doda, who did an X-rated song and dance revue in which she would stick the microphone into her vagina, would give Frankie a hard-on, in a dress.

Frankie missed his court date, which they dismissed anyway. They didn't want to see that pain in the ass again anyway. North Beach Revival was about to open, and Frankie got a position as a waiter, bus boy, bar back, and whatever else the kitchen gangsters and bar staff needed. The pad was glorious. It was the envy of all the neighbors and everyone who saw it. Kim and Frankie bought a 1960 Cadillac Fleetwood (with wraparound back window), twenty-seven thousand original miles, from an old Jewish couple who lived in Seacliff. They drove it to Reno once, but that was it. It sat in the garage. It was like brand-new—$400.

It was the later part of 1971 when the Iron Butterfly broke up, Muhammad Ali had his draft evasion conviction overturned, the Golden Gate Bridge was paid off, Apollo 15 landed on the moon, George Harrison's *Bangladesh* was released, John Lennon releases "Imagine," and Frankie was going to be eighteen.

The times were the greatest and most significant of any since the events that led to a new and brave new world that led into a new decade as important as the events of 1968; there was Frankie, riding the rocket into the future, and he was hanging on tight.

He had lived a lifetime in a mere couple of years and was an authority on matters of the cultural revolution and knew something about the political one. But now it was time to go back home and blow some minds—something he was an expert at doing.

Dressed in his best belled brown crushed velvet pants, silver shoes, tight-knit cotton shirt (with lightning bolts stitched into it), Rod Stewart haircut, two earrings, opal jewelry (conservative for his normal look), he was being kind and headed for Sacramento to see the family. He drove up to the house he and Arnie had worked so arduously on landscaping and painting an early modern design to grow into what now looked like a good idea. He got out of the Caddy; looked around like he just landed; walked up the Dichondra-bordered steps they'd poured years before, bamboo and ivy mounds to the sides, Japanese maples with leaves just turning; and entered the otherwise middle-class world now looking small. He knocked on the front door.

"Frankie!" said Joni as she leaped into his arms in a strong embrace. She kissed him and said, "Oh, you!"

Arnie came in the entry of the house and with more pain showing on his face gripped Frankie in a teary clutch, almost too forceful, and said, "Frankie, you're home." Everybody had been put through too much, and they were glad to just not have to think about it lying in bed at night. "You're just in time for dinner," Joni said tearfully.

"I told you I'd be back the day after my eighteenth birthday," said Frankie. They were not showing the pain they felt, nor did they have a grasp on who did what and who was to blame. It was Frankie who abandoned them, they figured, but kept it to themselves.

"So where did you go?" asked Arnie. "We didn't know what to think when we found your letter on the car last summer," added Arnie as they sat down for dinner.

"Boston," said Frankie.

"Boston?" said Arnie.

"That's right, Boston," said Frankie.

"How did you get all the way to Boston?" he asked.

"A plane, Dad, I took a plane." It was about then that Arnie put together that the kid had to have had some help getting to Boston; he didn't have the resources to get to Boston. They would have to tread lightly when it came to being the formerly not really abusive but degrading asshole that Arnie had been. He'd have to keep his demeaning self in check that he would have normally launched into like the old way of dealing with the kid.

"Kelly just kind of died when you left," Arnie had to say. She had to be put down for a broken heart. He did love that dog. That was Arnie's way of throwing a body blow and not making it such that Frankie would just walk out because there was no reason for putting up with that anymore. Arnie's words were designed to hurt, just like it always had been. Asshole. They trould never really understand why he left and always considered it something he did to them instead of the other way around. They did the best they could.

It was hugs and kisses goodbye. Frankie invited them to the City to visit; now it was time to see Betty.

The Admiral was history. Who knows why or where he was, but Betty could only say, "I thought you were dead in a ditch somewhere. How could you do that to me?" Frankie seemed to recall her smacking the shit out of him, which, with a smart mouth, he probably deserved, but then your asshole little sailor clubbing him, causing serious injury, might have had a little something to do with it. This kid grew up and could see right through the lies she told and believed. They did the best they could. Arnie was twenty and Betty was eighteen when they had Frankie. They were young and stupid—how unusual. Betty was invited to visit him in the City. She couldn't hurt him anymore.

His position at North Beach Revival expanded to one of enforcer (or assistant to the real enforcers). The band Aum was playing their great song "Mississippi Mud," and the lead guitarist and everybody else looked up at the ceiling to see tiles coming down onto the dance floor. The guitarist must have thought this was good, that he was responsible, but no, it turned out there was somebody up there. The bartenders, Tony and Gino, who were the muscle, got a look at the poor fool dumb enough to think he could hide up there and, once the place was empty, jump down and steal all the money, wherever that might be. Being the good soldiers that they were, they grabbed their guns and headed up to the roof. The guy could see he had been found out and was being pursued, so he ran across the rooftops eastward toward Montgomery Street. They were shooting at the poor motherfucker who had jumped down off the roof and was caught by the cops at Montgomery and Columbus when Frankie arrived on the scene. The cops had the guy on the ground, and he was saying, "These guys are shooting at me!" The cops were looking at each other, and the crowd was taking the whole thing more seriously. Tony handed Frankie the gun and told a couple who had just come from the club and given them a ride to take Frankie back to the club. They said okay, and the moment Frankie got in the back seat, a cop car pulled up behind them and turned on their lights. North Beach was very crowded, and it took getting through traffic and sitting at a couple of traffic lights to get back to the club. The guy pulled into the alley next to the club, and Frankie hopped out and ran into the club. The only thing that made sense was that the cops knew who they were dealing with by the location of the club and did nothing. He delivered the gun to Emile in the basement, and it may have very well been the same cops that Frankie had brought drinks to while they were on duty in the basement. They let him go, and Emile gave him a knowing smile as he took the gun when he came into the salad-making room, which Emile ran.

Frankie was now their little buddy. They liked the fact he put his ass on the line for them. Emile, master salad maker, said, "The best salad in North Beach." Frankie wasn't about to question it, especially after passing the salad room one night and Emile pulled a Luger out of his overcoat hanging on a coat rack, cocked it, and said, "You see what would happen if you don't do what I say." He had a big smile to let the kid know he was kidding.

Arnie and Joni actually came to the club one night from Sacramento to have dinner and see if any of it was actually true. It was true. Joni complemented "Bad News" on his dance steps. He was doing some kind of bump with Margo St. James. "Bad News." He was a very muscular black guy with a mohawk haircut and was part of Jefferson Airplane's security (he beat people up back stage at their concerts if they ever tried to get on stage). Margo St. James was head of COYOTE (Call Off Your Old Tired Ethics)—Prostitute's Union. The people who came to the "Revival" were movers and shakers in town. They got an eye full.

Frankie was working one night delivering drinks and plates of food to the tables around the dance floor, and at one of the tables was a redheaded beauty who had designs on Frankie. After a few cocktails and with very little fanfare, she made it clear she wanted to fuck his brains out. She was coming home with him. Her name was Glenda. She was trying to impress her girlfriends. That was okay with him. They didn't make it to the bedroom. She ripped his and her clothes off and climbed on for an exhilarating fuck on the living room floor.

Upstairs from the boys at Hermann Street lived a macho-looking shipyard worker. He ignored Frankie and Kim when passing in the stair hall and was not impressed with the way they looked, which kind of fascinated Frankie. Everybody had some sort of reaction to the clothes and the hair, but not this guy.

Robert was his name, and Frankie couldn't resist sticking his nose into the guy's business. "Wanna smoke a joint?" he asked one day as they passed in the hall.

"Sure, come on up," said Robert. The apartment above the boys was a penthouse with great views of the City and had been made into a studio, an art studio. Robert's rough exterior did not reveal the artist that he was.

"Outta sight. You're an artist?" said Frankie.

"Yeah," he answered. The unfinished paintings showed tools and equipment seen in a shipyard for doing work on ships. Small tractors, large propellers, rope, that kind of thing. Not very marketable, but cool. "What's this about?" he asked. "Just what you see. No more, no less." Frankie fired up a doob. He seemed glad someone was interested in his work, but he didn't offer any explanation for it. He could be mean to this kid and get away with it. "I study painting at the Art Institute," he said. "It's not finished," he added with a bite. "Beer?"

"Yeah, thanks," Frankie said. "Schlitz, Breakfast of Champions." He took the tall can and pulled the tab off. Robert just looked at him, took a pull off the joint, and said, "Yeah."

Glenda was now on Frankie's list of fuck buddies and conveniently lived nearby on Steiner and Hayes, across from the park, in one of the famous Victorian row houses looking down upon the Civic Center and all downtown San Francisco. She was a Midwest girl from Joliet, Illinois, and worked as a governess for a key figure in the music scene and key figure in the Avalon Ballroom and Family Dog. Gary was the behind-the-scenes operator and partner of Chet Helms, who he knew from Austin, Texas. It also turned out they were smugglers of grass from Mexico supplying the Haight Ashbury with the pot, very successfully. Everybody was smoking it, the good shit.

The Steiner Street house was large and spacious, furnished with authentic Victorian antiques, overstuffed couches, lace lampshades on turned walnut stands, and the trappings of a modern world gone by. Gary had the master bedroom; Glenda had the bedroom on the upper west side overlooking the park. Lilith, Gary's daughter, had the bedroom downstairs, and Michelle, from Lompoc, Glenda's best friend, had the other one next to hers. Gary's daughter was Glenda's responsibility, hence, being governess. Gary didn't have a clue how to take care of a little girl, and Glenda, as was her nature, took control of the situation and made sure she got fed, properly clothed, and ready for school. Frankie was there a lot because he grew to like Glenda, and free dope. Gary didn't much like Frankie. He had designs of his own on Glenda but could not act on them, being older, and Frankie was just a little to gay for someone from Texas.

Jim Morrison was dead in Paris at age twenty-seven.

North Beach Revival became a key venue for bands looking for recognition and a record deal. Santana, Jerry Garcia, and Merle Sanders, Alice Cooper (already on the map), Dr. Hook and the Medicine Show ("Got my picture on the cover of *Rolling Stone*"), Robert Shields (Mime, in the tradition of Marcel Marceau), and numerous other acts came through. Pete Marina (Warner Brothers Record Division) threw promotional parties with expensive presentations. The local gangsters came in to see the shows and get the best steak in North Beach. They all loved Frankie. He was a novelty but also one of them; he did their work with a smile.

Scott was still in charge of their interests, ran the club with a knowing smile and a sharp North Beach Leather shirt on. The broads loved him, and he got lots of poontang. One night Frankie drank too much, and Scott took care of him by including him in the journey home in his badass Mercedes sports car in the hills above Mill Valley with a hot stripper (he loved show girls) and held a big cool hand over the kid's forehead as he barfed up the evening's menu sitting on the steps to his garden and left him comfortably on the couch of his class pad while he gave it to the show girl good.

"You know where I can get some grass?" Robert asked one day.

"How much?" asked Frankie.

"How much is a half of a pound?" asked Robert.

"Two hundred fifty," said Frankie.

"Okay," he said. He knew he could get a half of a pound for $175 from Gary. He clinched the deal and made a few bucks learning the ropes. Bigger and better things were to come.

He got some Orange Sunshine acid, five hundred mics. He took it like it was no big deal. They were hanging out at the pad, and Pallop came over to visit Kim. Frankie thought it would be nice to take a walk; it was a nice day. He headed up to Buena Vista Park on the City side and found a patch of grass to lay on and look up at the sky and the view of the City.

As it got dark, the acid really hit him incredibly. He had taken plenty of acid, but nothing like this. The sky became a screen on which he watched the actual wavelengths of the light changing and going from light to dark, making patterns and patterns of color. John and Yoko were looking down upon him and helping guide him into the next move. He gave up ego and identity and found himself on Haight Street, just down the hill from Buena Vista Park. At that time, he had some kids run up to him on the corner of the liquor store on Haight and Stanyan and ask if he'd go in and buy them some beer. He said, "Sure." The kid gave him five bucks, and he went in and bought a six-pack of Budweiser, no questions asked. He gave the bag to the kid and didn't even think to ask for one. He was, after all, eighteen—too young to drink.

Haight Street was a ghost town. Everything was boarded up and closed. Even the Fish and Chips place that he and Ray used to eat at when they were in the City was gone. Dead.

He still didn't know who he was, where he was, or anything. He was on automatic—a state of being that was a result of conditioning and repetition that proved to get results. It happened. It was happening until he was wandering back and forth up Fifteenth Avenue at Irving Street. He felt the life force in each house as he walked as though he was breathing every breath himself, gesturing toward the sky, and noticed a couple of cops sitting in their car with heads leaning on their hands in disgust. The Irish Catholic neighborhood had good connections, not to mention those Irish grandmothers felt a little twinge when the strange fellow wandering down the street got all emotional and felt their feelings. Creepy, maybe. Who is that? Well-groomed but long hair, earrings, nice clothes. Acting too weird, though—better call the police. He had a three-quarter-length bear fur coat on. Hot, he took it off, folded up, and put it on a garbage can. Still hot, he took off his white ribbed wool sweater, folded up, and put it on the garbage can. The cops started their car drove up next to Frankie, got out, walked up to him, and said, "You wanna go home, or you wanna go to jail?"

"I wanna go home," he said. The cops took him to the Kezar station and put him in a cell. The jail was cold and dark. He sat there still not comprehending that he was in jail. He had no ego, no identity. After a couple of hours shivering in the cold dark holding cell, he realized he wanted out of there and started pestering the desk sergeant, demanding to make a phone call and began bugging him with questions he didn't want to be bothered with answering. The disgusted cop was tired of waiting for a wagon to come from downtown and get this goofy kid and certainly tired of the dumb questions from him and finally said, "I don't know. Get the hell out of here, go home," and let him go.

He had to ask him one last dumb question, and that was "Where was I picked up?"

"Fifteenth and Irving," he said. Frankie had about $2.43 to his name and got as far as he could in a cab and ran the rest of the way.

He was freezing his ass off. The Irish grandmother who called the cops was undoubtedly peeking out from behind the curtain and got a beautiful bear fur coat and nice wool sweater.

He wandered around aimlessly until he came upon a flooded Laguna Honda Boulevard. The entire road was like a river bottom. He had no idea what happened there, but he was sure he was on another planet. Wandering and wandering, he somehow came upon Hermann Street. He was home.

Kim was sitting there quietly reading a book, warm, safe, in a chair. He looked up at Frankie and said, "Where have you been?"

"You wouldn't believe it if I told you."

He was having a good time but really not getting anywhere at the Revival, so he got a job at the hip clothing store up on Grant Avenue, Water Brothers. These were the same people who owned Rainbow Cobbler on Columbus. They made the nicest custom (high-heeled, platformed) boots and shoes and also made custom shirts and velvet and satin coats, very nice and very expensive. It was frequented by rock musicians and movie stars. You would never know by his image, but Andy Williams came in one day and wanted to know how much a sculpture was. He had on a doeskin (North Beach Leather, you could always tell) suit with fringe and beads. The sculpture was eight mannequin heads with long tongues in rather contorted shapes sticking out (stupid looking, really). He had an entourage of people fussing over his every move. It was $2,000, but no one could reach the owner (who was a junkie), so there was no sale.

Edgar Winter came in and bought a lightweight leather suit with flashing lights (which was hard to pull off in 1972) that represented the flowers of a vine painted on it.

Red Fox from Sanford and Son came in one day and said, "Got any coke?" Frankie said he could get some later. "At the Hyatt, room 267, see ya before the show." Mick Jagger was cruising around in a white Rolls-Royce checking out San Francisco. It went on and on.

New York Dan was around. Too cheap to buy expensive clothes but was always on the lookout for pussy and see what Frankie was up to. He knew the parties and always managed to talk his way into getting in shows or back stages or gallery art shows for free. He dragged Frankie along to watch the master at work and show him the treasures he found. He did talk his way into some pretty interesting situations. Satty was a German artist who did some of the Avalon and Fillmore poster art. He had acclaim. His studio was on Filbert and Stockton in a storefront, downhill from the Art Institute. Good parties. The storefront was like a gallery, but downstairs in the basement was where all the drug-taking and consumption of alcohol happened. The Den of Iniquity was a round low table around which there were many very comfortable overstuffed chairs. The table was crowded with bottles of wine and liquor bottles, some with booze, some empty. He was a stiff German; everyone was so fucked up. He didn't like the black fingernails. He was a great artist, though. His work was basically a collage of pictures cut out of *National Geographic*s and all magazines with great content, silkscreened, printed, colorized, and was divvied up into different parts with different colors, etc. It was very unique art maybe. It was a formula he stuck to. He sold it. Frankie stole some of it.

A new gay nightclub opened where everyone was going after the other clubs closed at 2:00 a.m. Not sure it had a specific purpose of being a gay nightclub, just an after-hours club on Market Street near Castro.

It was named the Shed, and everybody from every club in the City soon found out it was an after-hours club and everybody would be there.

Frankie was there, and it was about 3:00 a.m., and there was movement to leave and on the way out to the front door. Up came a cutie from behind, put her arm through his, and said, "I want you to take me home." Frankie really didn't say much other than "Okay."

Vicki was a hot little number, wanted to be part of the scene. A local girl, she grew up in Daly City and became one of those friends, fuck buddies. She got it good that night and many after that.

She was a talented seamstress and maker of rock and roll clothing. She lived in Pacific Heights on Pacific Street in a nice, fancy building. Her roommate was a drug dealer from New York City who was there most of the time, so she had the place to herself. She had a king-sized water bed with black satin sheets. They got into the mushrooms that her absent roommate left her and would fuck all night long. What he really liked about her was she was almost hairless (underarms and vagina) naturally. He got her a job at Water Brothers as a seamstress. She had a room in back where she hemmed slacks and fit shirts and coats. She was very good at it.

As if that weren't enough, across the street from Water Brothers was an antique clothing store run by a beautiful black girl he actually knew from having gone in clothes shopping with Theda and Rainbow. Her name was Maggie. She dressed in the antique clothing and was stylin'; she was hot. Frankie would get to her later, when he had time to give her his undivided attention and a very hard dick.

Frankie answered the door one morning, and Robert said, "You want to go to Point Reyes?"

"You have a car, right?"

"Yeah."

"Where's Point Reyes?" asked Frankie.

"Not far," he said.

"You got money for gas?" asked Frankie.

"Yeah, I do. I got some acid too. You take acid, don't you?" he asked.

"Oh yeah, I take acid," said Frankie. Frankie, Robert, and Robert's long, tall California girl girlfriend Judy got into the '60 Cad and whooshed like the breeze across the Golden Gate bridge up 101 North to the San Anselmo exit to Dir Francis Drake Boulevard and headed toward Olema.

At Olema, they turned right and went to Bear Valley Visitor Center. Robert said, "We park here and walk." They got out and walked up the Bear Valley trail about a half a mile until they came upon a creek and a little bridge to the other side where sat a quaint Victorian yellow and white cabin. "Gordon," yelled Robert. A minute passed, and an all-American guy with long hair and a mustache came out on the porch and smiled when he saw the three of them. He pointed to the bridge, and they walked across it. "Hi, Gordon," said Robert.

"Hi, Robert," said Gordon.

"This is Judy, and this is Frankie," he said.

"Hi, come on in," said Gordon. The cabin was beautiful. He walked over to the screen door and opened it, gesturing for the trio to enter. In the warm glow was his beautiful wife and two daughters sitting at the kitchen table eating lunch. "This is Judy and my girls, Amy and Ansell," he said.

"Your name is Judy too?" said Ansell, the older daughter.

"Yes, it is," said Robert's Judy.

"You sure are a cutie-pie," said the other Judy.

"Have a seat. You want something to eat?" asked hostess Judy.

"That'd be great, thank you," said Frankie.

They were a quiet young hippie couple living for next to nothing in an unincorporated Point Reyes National Seashore cabin without electricity. Gordon and Robert worked together at Mars Aviation dismantling old planes, and Robert knew Gordon as a mechanical genius who put v-8s in motorcycles and Honda 350 engines in mini bikes in his Daly City youth. They went to the College of Marin in Mill Valley on student loans and raised their daughters in a beautiful place. Gordon powered their cabin by rotating the batteries of his '56 and '57 Chevys he ruled the roads in that area with.

Gordon entertained them with the new Pink Floyd record and got them in the mood for what was in store for tomorrow. That would be it for the night.

They rose early and had a breakfast of oatmeal and peaches. Robert put the hits of acid—how many and how strong not known—into a jug of Red Mountain Burgundy wine and began chugging it with glee. Robert, Judy, Gordon, and Frankie passed it around a couple of times. Gordon had the batteries rotated in the car, got it warmed, and readied for the day's adventure. A typical red-and-white model, it looked like a sleeper, but it was not. Gordon couldn't help but hot rod it, and he sure did. Otherwise cherry, it was muddy and with no back seats. The youngsters (Frankie and Judy) got the back floor. Gordon drove it extremely fast, and knowing the roads, they ripped up Highway 1 back past the Olema Country Store and toward Bolinas. In the section of Highway 1 before getting to the turnoff, it was very curvy. They were laughing and hanging on for dear life as the wine continued to get consumed that wasn't getting spilled as Gordon negotiated the course. They abruptly came upon an elderly couple in a flawless '68 T Bird, which had a cup holder with cups of coffee that had never been spilled, going very slow. Gordon passed them into a blind corner, almost getting into a head-on collision with a Marin County Sheriff's car coming the other way.

That made the whole adventure even funnier except the cop spun around and was now on their tail with lights flashing. Mesa Road was a dead end. Not that those rolling around in the back knew that, but Gordon did. The laughter died down when they could hear the siren wailing. Past the US Coast Guard installation (antenna farm) and the Bird Observatory, the cop was still with them. It was otherwise cattle ranches with barbed wire fences on both sides. Being very up- and down-like, one could see the cop was still in pursuit one hill back. With such terrain and at high speed, the wheels were coming off the road. They came down from one hill, and in front of them in the middle of the road was a big fat American station wagon right in the middle of the road with mom and dad and the kids who had never seen a cow before were waving to the bovines. Gordon somehow magically didn't even try to stop but passed them on the left with an embankment on his left and a quarter of an inch from their rearview mirror on the right. The cop had to slam on the brakes so as to not smash into them and kill everybody. They got to Palomarin Trailhead parking lot, spun into a spot, hopped out, and went running up the trail to Bass and Pelican lakes, five miles up the trail. The cop wouldn't wait, they hoped.

"Hippies came here not long ago in buses and set up teepees. There was an opium poppy growing right there after the cops kicked them out," said Gordon.

Nervously smiling as they made their way up the trail, looking back, they finally laughed and laughed. What a beautiful place—Central California Point Reyes. They were young and stoned on acid and walked past Bass Lake and Pelican Lake, and knowing where he was going, Gordon found Wildcat Creek, which led down to Wildcat Beach. Gordon, their fearless leader, chose a very iffy way down the creek to the beach. Not only was Judy ill-equipped to negotiate the creek that cut through the rock over the centuries, but Frankie had on a pair of turquoise painted boots, not meant for climbing, not really being useful footwear for descending down a waterfall that was chosen by Gordon to fall down in, and they fell down in it. They all fell down. They were not hurt, but it was funny to see. They laughed.

They reached Wildcat Beach healthy and very stoned, with smiles all around that they had averted disaster, and innocently bumbled their way to the beautiful totally secluded beach. The sun came out, and they watched a flock of pelicans soar over the waves in perfect unison without batting a wing. "You can almost see where their hands were, like their ancestors the pterodactyl," said Robert. "And you could see the homologous relationship pelicans had with the pterodactyl without the little hands."

They found the right trail to get them from the beach back to the main trail and back to the parking lot. On the way, they saw full-grown deer with spots, white ones, black ones. Trippy. Gordon told them that Bing Crosby owned the property at one time and was going to put a golf course there as well as a game reserve for him and his buddies to hunt and had it stocked with exotic deer.

They made it back by dark. They didn't realize just how far they had gone, but it was a long way. They were tired and hungry and completely forgot about the cop, who fortunately forgot about them.

Vicki brought a young nymph by the name of Angel around the store. She was a seamstress too. Not that there was enough work for one, but she also had some sort of relationship with Pete, Vicki's roommate—Panhandle Pete. Frankie had yet to meet him since he was in New York, but Angel didn't hold him in such high regard, saying, "He gets so mad sometimes." She was a cutie-pie. She was a small girl, probably from Italian dissent, with brown eyes, big tits, and had a hippie child look that exuded sex.

She somehow gained access to Vicki's bedroom when she and Frankie were having a mushroom-fueled all-nighter on the satin sheets. She was on the floor watching them longingly, just peeking above the bed while Vicki shooed her away. "Go away, Angel," said Vicki.

"She just wants to watch. What's wrong with that?" said Frankie. How was she here, unless Vicki wanted her there? Frankie would make time for Angel later. At the time, Frankie was pretty busy with Vicki's almost hairless pussy.

The Stones had just released *Exile on Main Street* and were in town playing at Winterland. Five shows, two a night. Frankie and Vicki made it to at least three. She made a killer rock and roll shirt with a long silk fringe on the sleeves. She actually made it for Pete, but Frankie gave it a real workout ripping it up with Mick. Great shows. Frankie was a rock star.

Water Brothers was a fun place to work, but the owner was a junkie and would come in and empty the cash register in a hurry and split without saying anything. Getting paid began to be a problem. Of course, Frankie spent most of his money on clothes anyway, so money was inconsequential. There was never a problem. But the time had come to get a real job. Frankie was going to get a job as a cabinetmaker, something he knew a little about, his uncle having been one.

He answered an ad and met with Paul and Richard, a gay couple who had a shop on Capp and Seventeenth Streets. They made very simple, very cool furniture that they sold on Polk Street at their store, New Dimensions. Frankie would start work with them as an apprentice.

Paul was older and the brains of the operation. He was a jovial short bald guy with a good heart. Richard, Paul's lover, was Latin, conceited, arrogant, and listened to opera, maybe to erase his Mexican roots and become something other than. But he was pretty much of a prick and treated Paul like shit. They had custom-sized parsons tables, pedestals, displays, those kinds of things for their store and furniture places in the bay area. It paid pretty well. Frankie adapted well and liked the routine.

Kim worked in Berkeley at the North Gate selling flowers for Pallop. He would either pick him up after work or walk from Hermann Street or Steiner Street. It wasn't far.

Angel was dying to fuck Frankie and finally picked a night he wasn't busy, but Frankie was such a slut that he finally got the clap. It wasn't Glenda. It was probably Vicki; he didn't know. Unfortunately, Glenda was at the pharmacy on Market Street when Angel was buying a contraceptive and said to Glenda, "I'm on my way to see Frankie." Glenda, Frankie's official girlfriend, didn't like hearing that, especially knowing he had the clap, another source of irritation, because it wasn't her. "You're going to see Frankie, right now?" she asked.

"Yep, see ya," she replied and pranced out of the store. How they knew each other was a mystery to Frankie.

"I have the clap, baby," said Frankie as he answered the door.

"What does that mean?" she asked.

"Well, we can't fuck, but we can still have some fun," he said.

"Okay," she said. She had high heels and black stockings on (a trick Panhandle Pete must have schooled her on or somebody). It was unclear whether she was even eighteen, but he didn't ask. She got naked except for the shoes and stockings, sat down on the bed, and spread her legs. She could get his nut by jacking him off furiously and then again. Nice to be young and virile. He gave up about a quart of jizz. It made him think of the name of the shirts at Water

Brothers, Jizz. He devoured her sweet young hairy pussy. He got the bush out of the way to get the pink button. Not sure if she got her nut. She sure was young and sweet, though.

Frankie had the means to have clothes made of his design (by the same shop that made Water Brothers clothes) and did not give up the nightlife in North Beach even though by day, he was a dusty woodworker with his nose to the grindstone. There was plenty of stepping out to do, being a rock star, with a devoted girlfriend, Glenda. They made all the parties and major concerts at Winterland. Having connections, they got backstage passes as well as recording sessions with Texas musicians. Doug Sahm (Sir Douglas Quintet) was among them. Gary produced his record on which Bobby Dylan played on. "Is anybody going to San Antione?" and "Mendocino, Mendocino," was a better-known track. He was always hanging around the Steiner Street house. The principles from KSAN were around. Chet was there. Not sure what he did. He later was informed as to what Chet did prior to that time, but Frankie only knew he hung around, smoked a lot of dope, and just laid back with his German shepherd, Foot. He was a very nice, gentle person.

It was said that Chet was responsible for bringing Janis to town, but the inside scoop was that actually, Julius was the guy. Frankie didn't know, but he did know that Julius was Gary's right-hand man and the guy who actually got stuff done. All Frankie knew was he was a man on the run all the time.

He looked into a box sitting on the floor at Steiner Street to see the 5x7-inch colored Avalon and Family Dog posters. Great art at the time and still great art. They knew it, and Frankie knew it too. He helped himself to a few, no reason to be greedy. This was history. He'd have to tell his story someday.

Glenda and Frankie grew closer and closer. The sex was good. He still wanted to fuck every cute girl in sight, though. Glenda was certainly free to do what she wanted; it was understood. He did respect her feelings and showed her respect. He didn't want to hurt her feelings. She was stable, being a governess and all, and created order.

Robert and Frankie hung out in his penthouse studio, smoking Kools and drinking Schlitzes, Robert's permanent diet. He was thoughtful and intellectual and gave Frankie the benefit of his insight, and liked being mean to Frankie. He had issues, but it just rolled off Frankie's back, which fascinated Robert even more. Maybe Frankie wasn't just an empty vessel, a shallow pretty boy with silver shoes and no depth of character. Maybe the acid was having an effect, and there was something there. "Like giving acid to a grasshopper," he would say and laugh. That image really amused him. That wasn't this.

Gordon and Robert hatched a plan that backfired on them. With all the free love and sexual activity swirling around decided, they were going to sleep with each other's Judys and have an orgy. Robert, of course, was silent about the failed experiment, but Frankie gathered from bits of information about the event that the Judys learned they were lesbians and wanted each other more than they wanted Robert and Gordon. Frankie thought it was pretty funny. It ended their relationships, kids and all.

Gordon's daughter Amy somehow got left in the care of Robert and Frankie. They went for a walk up to Twin Peaks, quite a hike. The three of them walked and walked; they had to carry Amy a little bit on their shoulders. They made it and took in the great view and headed on back down the hill. She was a little doll, and the two men were making sure she was happy and having a good time. It was sweet; they had fun.

Work was going well for Frankie. He was learning a lot from Paul about woodworking and finishes. Everybody needed something built.

Frankie and Vicki would drift apart. More than drift apart, he was with Glenda. He still didn't meet Panhandle Pete. For all Frankie knew, Pete and Vicki were boyfriend and girlfriend, knowing Vicki, the little slut. But again, there were no rules. Everybody did whatever they wanted.

The year 1972 was an important year. George Harrison released the film and album *Concert for Bangladesh*. He was always his favorite Beatle, and his compassion for the starving people made him cry when he watched the film. He set the standard for people helping people around the world. John and Yoko hosted *The Mike Douglas Show*. It was a new era. Nixon was visiting China. As much of a dick he was, that was significant, in time of the cold war.

Everybody and his brother, the US, Russia, and France were setting off nukes. The stupid frogs set one off in the South Pacific, and the fallout drifted into Australia. Apollo 16 landed on the moon, Giant's traded Willy Mays to the Mets, David Bowie hit the scene with *Ziggy Stardust*. Nixon and Haldeman used the CIA to cover up Watergate; the newly liberal Supreme Court ruled that the death penalty was "cruel and unusual" punishment. American troops left Vietnam. "Peace is at hand," said Henry Kissinger.

But the highlight of the year was Stanley Kubrick's *Clockwork Orange*. Robert and Frankie went to see it. Robert literally looked like the little man standing on his chair clapping, and he was. The culture was straining to achieve a new level of departure from tradition; there were no holds barred. "Spare some cutter, me brother," said the burn in the underground tunnel as Alex and his droogies beat the shit out of the old man for fun. It was perverted, like the culture it mocked, but they knew not what they mocked.

On top of the world, Frankie visited the family in Sacramento. Brother Dana wanted some pot, so Frankie gave him a joint. He thought back to when he gave him acid on Christmas when he was ten. He sure did have a good time opening his presents. Frankie had to wonder whether having done that had somehow changed him into the greedy, self-serving little prick he had become. When Arnie caught him with the joint, rather than show any loyalty, he said, "Frankie gave it to me." Of course, dinner was actually like a trial. Arnie had to be the complete asshole he had always been and just laid it on a little too thick. His pain from Frankie having left and stayed away all that time became part of his attack on Frankie at the dinner table. He just couldn't see that he was the reason Frankie left. No, it was Frankie's fault. He did that to them. Arnie would never accept that he might have had something to do with it. Blind.

Frankie finally said, "Fuck this, I'm outta here," got up, walked out the door, got in the Caddy, and left. It would have been nice to have someone who was on the same side as him, a common enemy they could fight together. Frankie was the enemy. But he was now free.

Living between Steiner Street and Hermann Street, life was good. The job was good, the money was good, and there was more poontang and psychedelia than he could handle. He was well-dressed, pretty smart—the future was bright.

At the apartment on Hermann Street on one shiny day, Frankie was not up to much, so he took some nice acid. KSAN was on (Kim's rich mother paid for the top-of-the-line Pioneer receiver), and they had just gotten the live version of Jimi Hendrix's performance at Woodstock. Wow! Of course he had died and was no longer with them, but turning the live recording up to maximum volume became one with Jimi. He became overwhelmed with his presence and even became a vessel for Jimi. He became Jimi—scared the shit out of him. There was no mistake. "The Star-Spangled Banner" was what put it over the top.

Vicki came back into the picture by contacting him and letting him know Pete had come to town and was here to stay. He went over to the apartment to meet him. He was a normal fellow, tall, brown hair, Kentucky graduate, English. Smart, full of himself—who cared? Not Frankie. Pete never did anything without a reason. He wanted to meet the local young bucks with connections and sold dope. His dope. He was a member of the Hog Farm. Wavy Gravy was their most well-known "breakfast for four hundred thousand," he announced at Woodstock. They were famous for having buses and showed up at all the major concerts around the country and every Grateful Dead concert. "Everybody should take acid at least once in their life," Pete would say.

The Berkeley Barb was the voice of radical student body. It had the kind of moral authority of the movement (at least they thought so). The December edition in 1972 had articles that started as follows: "A Shrink Is a Shrink." R. D. Laing spewed irrelevant hippy garbage for two hours at UC Berkeley Tuesday night, and an SRO audience of middle-class students and assorted guru worshipper types at Zellerbach Auditorium ate it up. Imagine that, even R. D. Laing wasn't hip enough for them. Nick Benton (whoever the fuck he was) was the author. The vile rag slammed everybody in government and political life for not being moral enough (for them). In the back, it advertised, "Preteen sex, Scandinavian Import Co., and beautiful Mexican girls needing American boyfriends" and "Take your own pictures of nude models at the Photographers Studio." They were selective about who was exploited, but it was okay for them because they were hip.

The skewed justice was at an all-time high and skewed the other way from what had been in play just a few years before. The world was turned on its head, and the world accepted it. It was like the masses wanted to break out of the norm and let their hair down, so they went along with the extremist trend toward radicalism associated with the cultural revolution dancing to the beat of rock music. Not just students and hippies were opposed to the war, but moms and dads were too.

Frankie finally hooked up with Maggie, the black beauty who ran the antique clothing store on Grant Avenue. She sure did have style; she was hot and liked white boys. And Frankie was a white boy. He would visit her every once in a while at her beautiful apartment out in the Avenues. He had to watch out that she didn't scratch the shit out of his back, digging her fingernails into it while he gave it to her hard. They would see one another, and that went on for years.

Otherwise, he was mostly living at Steiner Street and occasionally made a pit stop at Hermann Street. He didn't concern himself with rent or things like that. One night he stopped by to find the lock had been changed and the key didn't work. He knocked on the landlord's door, and out came Charles, the owner. Charles came after him and was trying to choke poor Frankie. Rather than let Charles get his hands on him, he stepped aside, and Charles went tumbling down the stairs. Like he had seen before, as if planned, Ernest, his lover, was in a robe and had a frying pan in his hand that he was going to hit Frankie with. Frankie stepped aside and gave him a push as he came at Frankie, and down the stairs he went. He was naked under the robe, and Frankie was embarrassed for him when his very small uncircumcised penis, kind of red too, like he had been playing with it too much, was exposed, something Frankie really didn't want to see. Robert and Frankie called him Ernst.

Frankie never did ask why Kim didn't pay the rent that month. Maybe he thought he would just go away and leave behind the furniture and decorations and everyone would think Kim created all of this.

As cool of an apartment that it was, it was time to go. The next night, Frankie went by to start the process of moving. Out of Charles and Ernst's door came a butch former Marine friend of theirs (they had to have been sucking his dick) who was trying to get his meaty hands on Frankie. The tactic of using the aggressor's anger against him didn't quite work this time, and the Marine got a grip on Frankie. When it came down to it, they had each other in a grasp, but Frankie was still strong enough to get away from the guy and get upstairs. "You sonofabitch!" he said. It was time to go.

Paul and Richard had a house on Twenty-Sixth and Church Street in Noe Valley. It was owned by Bill and Silvia Cromwell. They had a Victorian on the corner and owned the not as fancy turn-of-the-century building next to it. They knew Paul because he was wheeling and dealing in antiques, brass lamps, that sort of thing. They had a corner antique store that had just about everything you could imagine. A counter in front and a couple of barber chairs that were usually occupied and, if not, invited you to come sit down and talk. Homes of Charm it was called.

Through Paul's introduction, he got the pad—three bedrooms, living room, dining room, big kitchen, attic the entire size of the place (70×20 feet), backyard. It was $185 a month.

There was room for Glenda and Michelle, her best friend, and all the things that incorporated homemaking, and of course, there was an archery range in the attic, which was something Frankie did in his youth.

The first order of business was, of course, the paint job. It was tall and Victorian, without the frills. The entry and hallway got painted charcoal gray with orange trim. The bedrooms got the trim painted black and turquois, the living room dark green, and the dining room blue and red. The kitchen was yellow, so the trim and floor got burgundy. There was a freestanding cutting table with chemical storage jars of grains and granola. It helped that Paul had lived there, was a furniture builder, and rather than move a bunch of stuff, like the cutting table, he and Richard just gave it to Frankie.

Hanging plants were in practically every room, and there were weights and sports equipment in his room—all the elements of a past he wanted to hang on to and a present he possessed and a future he would create. It didn't intimidate him.

Arnie called, and he wanted Frankie to come to San Mateo, where his lifelong buddy Ron Brazil lived. They called him Raz. He got a job for the company building BART. When Frankie was a kid, Raz would usually come screeching up to the house in a car (he had a little Metropolitan for a while), stop, get out, come to the front door, open it, step in, and start singing a Portuguese love song at full volume. He was always hammered. One time he did that, and the babysitter and Frankie just looked at him until he stopped and said, "Frankie, Where's your dad?"

"Not home."

"Oh," he said. Frankie should come down there and see Ron and Ruthie (his school teacher's wife whom Frankie always liked) and see what he had to say about Frankie getting a job as a carpenter (union), a good opportunity.

Frankie and Glenda took the Caddy down to San Mateo. It was on top of the hill with a view, big bucks. Arnie was debating leaving his lifelong job with the state—very secure, very steady—to come to the South Bay to work on BART also. He had engineering and administrative experience in the Department of Water Resources.

He hadn't seen them in a long time so they had to get reacquainted. They had drinks. The men went downstairs to play some pool and a game of chess; the women stayed in the kitchen and prepared dinner. Frankie beat Raz at pool. Time for a game of chess. Raz was drinking whiskey and got pretty fucked up and got beat at chess. He unraveled to the point of calling Frankie a fag. "Arnie, this guy is a fag," he said.

"I don't know, maybe. Why do you care so much?" said Frankie.

"The guys on the job would take one look at him and say, 'Hey, honey, come here. I wanna fuck you. They'd laugh him off the job,' he said.

"Why do you care so much?" Frankie said a second time. *Why would he care?*

When Frankie was young, Raz would come over in one of his drunken states and want to box. Frankie liked boxing him because he was such a loser. Frankie would *ratta, tat, tat*—fast jabs off the forehead and circle around and around, making the drunk dizzy. He did actually know how to box and would let the kid get the better of him for a while then step in and throw a real blow, usually knocking the kid on his ass. They had history.

Arnie was in tears. He said, "He doesn't know, he said he didn't know." He knew; he just let him think he didn't know, just to fuck with him.

He had a couple of boys about eight and ten and said, "You touch my boys and I'll kill you." Dinner was ready, but before they got to the table, Frankie had the boys stand behind the couch while he sat in it and put his arms around their shoulders behind him and had Glenda take a picture. The women got wind of what happened and let Ron know he was in deep shit with them until he apologized to Frankie. Like a bad dog, he apologized.

Ron called the kid the next day and apologized again and said he would get him a job with the company without a problem, sorry. Frankie declined but got a laugh out of the whole thing.

There was plenty experience playing house, and Glenda and Michelle knew what they were doing. Glenda was going to trade school to learn to do secretarial work, and Michelle worked at a shoe store on Polk Street owned by Bobby Bols, a man about town. He also owned the Paradise Lounge across the street, which was a bar that had his antique motorcycle collection displayed up high around the place. It was also a music venue. It was not very big, but he crammed maybe two hundred people into it. It was pretty happening. Kim was left with the empty apartment and needed Frankie to get through. He was a spoiled Korean rich kid who really didn't know how to take care of himself, having everything done for him by his grandpa's staff of servants.

He let Kim come around and let him stay in the attic from time to time. He was still doing coke, snorting. He had the means to pay for it, so he was at risk for getting strung out. It was a way to let him get out his shell he had lived in by being overprotected. He was at risk but super secretive. Frankie didn't know what was going on with him but let him stay when he needed it.

Bill and Silvia weren't just owners of the building and the antique store but had been former journalists and had lived in Hong Kong writing for a Western newspaper. Bill had written an article exposing the fact that the United States used nerve gas in a conflict in Taiwan. They somehow got swept up in the McCarthy era witch hunt and were blacklisted, and he wasn't sure to what extent they were persecuted, but they hated the American government and were in fact socialists, which was kind of dangerous. They passed on their hatred for the government to their three sons. John, the oldest, was a couple of years older than Frankie and went to a city college to supplement his hatred with political science and civics studies. Tom, who was about Frankie's age, lived in Bolivia and hadn't been seen in a while. Cam, the youngest, was a cowboy in training and a hunk but kind of stupid and not really that with it.

John lived downstairs in an impromptu but very cool and earthy apartment below Frankie's kitchen and carried on the family tradition of hating the American government. Frankie had a chess set sitting front and center in the living room. John was a chess player.

"Look at these colors. That's going to be hard to cover up," he said as he came in to investigate what was going on.

"This is Glenda," said Frankie, introducing him to her.

"Pleased to meet you. Nice piece, where did you get that?" he asked about a '30s chest of drawers in his bedroom.

"A friend in Oakland," said Frankie.

"Well, we'll have to play chess sometime," said John.

"Oh yeah, if you live downstairs, we will," said Frankie.

Frankie bought a pink '59 Cadillac for $300 and still had a share of the '60 Cad, which either Glenda or Kim drove. The piece-of-shit '62 Valiant that Gary gave Glenda was on its last leg. Life at the woodshop was good. Upstairs in the warehouse on Capp Street was a gay artist renting loft space. He was a painter. He stood in front of large canvasses and with corresponding colors slopped the paint up and down, side to side, up and trown, side to side. It had a depth of sorts, if you slopped enough strokes in reds, blues, greens, up and down, back and forth. It did create a modern sort of mess. The guy was selling paintings. It made Frankie think of Robert, who was a skilled artist, working in a shipyard.

Richard, Paul's Mexican lover boy, was just too much of an asshole for Frankie to put up with anymore and pissed him off enough that he just walked out one day. Just a block away on Seventeenth and Valencia was a woodshop that Paul had actually started with a guy he thought might have been his former lover. How he could be anybody's "lover"—totally did not make sense to Frankie. Richard was his name too. He was a tall lanky Texan and a stoned alcoholic covered in dust, and usually he had a booger hanging out of his nose and smoked a Benson and Hedges 100. He was now the sole proprietor of the Woodworkers Coop. Right on Seventeenth, with a big sign, got plenty of business. He couldn't imagine how he and Paul could have ever had a relationship and didn't even want to know. Paul was a sharp businessman and had started the place and walked away to do his own thing right down the way on Capp Street. The Coop was busy.

"Hey Richard, need another guy?"

"Yeah, I could use another guy. Not working with Paul anymore?"

"No, Richard is too difficult," said Frankie. "Great, I'll be here tomorrow."

It was a hot and sunny day. Frankie decided to go to Devils Slide, a nude beach just south of Pacifica. He picked up a gay hitchhiker in the 60, on the way to the popular gay nude beach. Stoned on acid, Frankie was wide-eyed and smiling. There were fortunately some naked women running around playing in the water, so he had some nice tits and ass to admire while his gay friend, who stuck with him for the ride back, was getting an eyeful of some very tan and very well-endowed gay boys playing volleyball. It was a beautiful day on the central California coast.

Just down the beach from them was an older (maybe thirty) Mexican dude, lying on a blanket, naked, with two short fat senoritas on both sides of him. They were stuffed into girdles and fancy Mexican underwear. They leaned over to him and talked nasty to him. His dick would swell up, get hard, and he'd shoot a load on his stomach. The two women would giggle and wipe up the spermato-zoa and put it all over themselves like suntan lotion. They did that over and over. Muchacho must have shot a couple of quarts. The gay guy said, "What a male chauvinist pig!" Frankie thought it was kind of cool, and the giggling senoritas certainly enjoyed it. They never touched his dick.

Frankie was dealing Pete's mushrooms that he began to think were store-bought mushrooms with acid added to it. And not enough—they didn't do much. Pete was an opportunist who knew what this shit actually was. Frankie wasn't impressed. Pete would make a lot of money, and Frankie was beginning to understand how. He was getting pot from Gary and Julius. He and Glenda became the focus of attention, and all kinds of people started coming around to hang out, listen to music, get high.

The nightlife was still calling, and answer it they did. Stepping out was high on the list of things to do, and they found themselves in the network of similarly minded young and beautiful people. Parties at Bimbo's, North Beach Leather parties at the Savoy Tivoli on Grant Avenue and parties at recording studios in South of Market in hidden alleyways. Doing coke became more and more common, but no more than a gram or so at a time.

Robert had moved out of the Hermann Street penthouse and got a quaint little dumpy house in Brisbane. He hooked up with an interesting little Scottish lady, Adrianna. He had a Taylor Topper, and she worked for the downtown San Francisco salon, where they do the fabricating and fitting of the toupee. The crummy little house was okay. They took acid to break it in.

The Coop was a good-sized shop with probably five guys. Four on the bench and one doing the millwork. The back was rented out to a couple of guys who were making wood toys that they sold at craft fairs and on Union Street. Richard's number one guy was a big Samoan named Malie. He carried the place on his back. He could do anything and was fast at doing it. Paul had hired him years before the guy kept coming around and wouldn't take no for an answer; he wanted to work there, and that was that. Paul had no choice but to hire him, and they were lucky they did. He showed Frankie the ropes. He loved to smoke pot, so Frankie was his buddy and sold him his "shit."

Church Street was hip, domestic bliss. Frankie and Glenda both had strong personalities and often butted heads and once in a while were jealous. It was agreed that they had an open relationship—in other words, they could fuck other people.

Probably through Gary and Julius, a blonde stud from out of town picked Glenda upon his fully dressed Harley, and they went on an all-day ride. They returned that night, and the guy looked spent and didn't feel like riding to wherever he was going. He left the Harley and got picked up by a chocolate brown Mercedes 230 convertible—expensive. Drug money. She had the distinct look of someone who had been fucked hard.

So when Glenda's sister came to visit a couple of weeks later from Illinois and Glenda went to the store, Frankie didn't feel so bad about giving it to her in John's apartment, who was in India. Diane was a clone of her sister with long brown hair and horny as hell. "Is there someplace we can fuck?" she asked.

"Downstairs, I'll be there in a minute," said Frankie. He went down to find her naked with legs spread and very wet, and Frankie, already hard, drove it in, driving her crazy and having her climb on, humping frantically. "Oh, oh, oh, oh, yeah, yeah, yeah, yeah, I'm coming, I'm coming, I'm cooooooommmmmmmmmmiiinnnnggg!" she screamed as Frankie shot a hot load into her. It took about thirty seconds.

He never once stopped to think about how planting his seed here and there, without protection, might have sprouted some human beings, as in babies. Children he would never know he had. His sperm was getting around, no doubt about it. He just figured the broad had to be taking the pill, but he didn't ask. The sex was too good to be asking pesky questions that would dampen the mood.

Brisbane was a wonderful country environment, with horses and an event known as Western Days. The town folk had the largest rotisserie in the Western world behind Demarco's 23 Club. It held six hundred chickens or a whole buffalo. They had the big parade every year until the Hells Angels took it over and ruined it for everybody.

They had to cancel it after they showed up. They just caused too much trouble, and Brisbane was a one-sheriff town at the time.

Tough John was a local figure whose dad owned the only gas station in town for the last thirty-five years. John was an ace mechanic, a man about town. He grew up there, knew everybody, was a hot rodder with a fully blown '57 Chevy that almost didn't idle, and had the smartest German shepherd known to man named Cuba. He would come over to Robert and Adrianna's house and drink vodka and grapefruit until he got extremely fucked up and passed out, while Robert and Frankie were just coming on. He amused them, and he found something in them he liked before he got too smashed. Tough John was the genuine article. Robert and Frankie kind of liked rednecks. They weren't that different; they were rednecks in their own way.

On the party circuit was Antonio, friend and partner of Panhandle Pete. Antonio was a charming Salvadorian fellow with self-taught good manners and had a way with beautiful women. He was an early fixture in the Haight Ashbury and knew a lot of people. He was part of a very early theater group, the Magic Theater. He studied Flamenco dance and had a regal air about him. He never said much but took plenty of acid and had a knowing look on his face. He and Frankie would have a lifelong friendship, not to mention share numerous women, hot women.

Robert drank a lot and discovered black beauties and drank even more. Being absent or late too many times at his Bethlehem shipyard job, he got fired. He took Frankie upon his invitation to come check out the Coop. "Hey, Frankie, what are you doing?" he said, surprising Frankie with his presence. He was working on the table saw, cutting table and bookcase parts to send to the guys on the benches by the open garage door on Seventeenth Street shop. "Hey, what's happening?" he said.

"So this is the Coop?" said Robert.

"Let me show you around and introduce you to Richard," said Frankie. As Frankie was showing Robert around, Richard came out of the office in a dusty cloud. Richard drank sometimes all night long and looked like it. "Richard, this is my good friend Robert."

"How do you do?" they said and shook hands. Robert was smoking a Kool and threw it on the ground and stamped it out, but it didn't go out and began burning the dust on the floor. They looked down at the smoldering black dust, and Robert embarrassingly stamped it out. It didn't faze Richard, who was mumbling something about how the shop worked. In the back of the shop was an unused corner that caught Robert's eye. "So you rent space to people who do their own thing," asked Robert.

"Yeah, we do," said Richard.

"I would be interested in renting this space in the corner," said Robert.

"Can I give you a hundred dollars a month for it?" said Robert.

"Yeah, we can do that," said Richard.

Glenda finished her courses at the trade school and wasted no time getting a job on the Twenty-Fifth Floor of One California building downtown. She was a go-getter and would succeed at anything she did, but living with Frankie and setting up house was not one of the things she would succeed at, through no fault of her own.

Glenda was sadly out of the picture for the time being. Frankie just wanted too much, and Glenda was a hindrance to the freedom he sought. Dumb mistake on his part, and she was really hurt by the breakup. Frankie would always call on her for sympathy fucks. She would soothe his restless mind when his behavior got out of control.

One night, he was stoned on acid and for whatever reason had been on an emotional roller coaster—because of the breakdown of the relationship with Glenda? He just didn't know.

It was free love, and they were so liberated none of it bothered them, but actually it did. He was a scoundrel and he knew it, no matter what the culture told him the way it should be. He was free, but maybe being that free wasn't so good—until the next hot piece of ass came along.

He was at *The On Broadway*, watching the music, scoping it out, his usual routine, sitting in the back. In front of him were three blondes sitting at a table, having some drinks and watching the show on stage. One got up and walked toward the front of the club, where the restrooms were. She was tall and elegant and moved with grace and purpose. He didn't even see her face but was so enchanted by her movement he ran after her. She turned around—what an innocent beauty. The lovely young woman looked surprised but happy to be getting the attention. He said, "What's your name?"

"Who are you?"

"Where are you going?"

"To the restroom. I'll be back in a minute," she said.

"I'll wait here," he said. She came out, and Frankie gathered himself up and put on a cool demeanor he knew he must show if he wanted to get anywhere with this beauty. "What's your name?"

"Mimi," she said.

"Frankie, can I buy you a drink?" he asked.

"Okay," she said.

Glenda was at Steiner Street, so after the show, Frankie talked to Mimi and her sister, Cybil—also a beauty with huge cans, with an admirer in tow—and her friend Naomi to come to his house. Three hot blondes.

They were reluctant but agreed. They knew what these wolves had in mind and put up a half-hearted resistance so as not to seem too easy.

Frankie just wanted to get Mimi into the sack, and she couldn't put up enough of a fight and finally gave in. She was barely eighteen, and Cybil was sixteen. They lived in Berkeley with their very permissive mother who was actually out there more than her daughters when it came to making babies with strange men. Fortunately, they were trust fund babies. Dad, who had divorced the crazy wife, an architect, did okay. But crazy mom's dad was a multi-multimillionaire, and none of his children ever worked and were all consequently neurotic as hell.

They had a nice house in the Berkeley Hills and liked to party, what else? She was not especially good in bed, but that was understandable with all the distractions. Frankie was a gentleman and gave up being too pushy; he would take his time with this one.

The year 1973 was a year of adjustment that came along with the change in American society. Nixon claimed to have reached an accord to end the Vietnam war, members of the American Indian movement began occupation of Wounded Knee, Marlon Brando turned down Oscar for the *Godfather* in support of the Indians, Jerry Garcia got busted for LSD, Nixon refused to release Watergate tapes, France was still setting off nukes in the South Pacific, Nixon released tapes with eighteen-minute gap, Rose Mary Woods said she accidentally caused it. A US psychiatrist said homosexuals were not mentally ill, and *The Exorcist*, starring Linda Blair, premiered. Most people were getting stoned and didn't care too much about world events, even though Watergate had everybody's attention. Nixon was a crook after all and was going down. Paul Krassner's insignificant little rag *The Realist* was the first to break the story. It took the straight press months to pick up on it and discover it was, in fact, a conspiracy.

What was really important was that Frankie was alone at Church Street. He got a roommate named Anna. She was a Latina, girlfriend of his friend Donny. Donny owned a restaurant called the Good Karma on the corner of Eighteenth Street and Dolores that Frankie ate at often. They had steamed veggies and brown rice with tamari—delicious.

She sold imported clothing and goods from South America and Mexico at street fairs and at shops around town. Upon her return from South America, she brought back six eight-millimeter film canisters for an acquaintance and put them on the television set in the living room. The acquaintance was supposed to come by to pick them up at some point.

John, who lived downstairs, was around and would come up and smoke a joint from time to time and talk about how great India was. "Want to play some chess?" he asked one afternoon as he walked in the back door without knocking. "Sure, let's play," said Frankie and headed into the living room. Frankie put on a Paul Butterfield record, which John liked, and they played. Frankie considered himself pretty good at chess but started to realize he was not as good as John. It wasn't that John was much better; he made a bad move, but he had Frankie psyched out. Frankie lost the first game, the second, and the third. Oh well, he'd get him next time.

Frankie was on Polk Street at the shoe repair shop having his shoe guy Tony (Italian of course) getting some stacked leather heels made for a pair of Al Green shoes, and prancing across the street was an elegant beauty with a lacey feminine sheer dress blowing in the breeze as she held on to her large white hat with ribbons blowing in the breeze. While traffic stopped to take a look, she was headed Frankie's way, into the shoe repair shop. "Hi."

"Hi." Frankie finished his business with Tony. "Thank you, Tony, see you."

"Thank you, Mr. Frankie," he replied as he raised his eyebrows after looking at the beautiful creature in his shop. "Like to have a cup of coffee?" he asked.

She looked and liked what she saw. "Okay, I have to meet someone at the Fairmont, though. Is that all right?" she said.

"That'll be fine," he said. "I'm Frankie, you are?" He stuck his hand out, palm up.

"Dhindi." She smiled and took his hand. They crossed Polk and walked up California Street. As they walked up California at Larkin, she pointed to an old multiunit apartment building. "This is where me and my mother live. I have to meet my mother and the owner at the hotel bar," she said. "Mrs. Stills? You've probably heard of Steven Stills."

"That's interesting," he said.

They got to the hotel bar, and Mrs. Stills had belted back about three martinis and was feeling no pain but was complaining about something undecipherable as Dhindi's mother gave a look to Dhindi of "Thank God you're here." Dhindi's mom had a stroke and a speech impediment. Dhindi was certainly a sweet lady, having to cope with a wealthy overbearing, ill-mannered drunk woman. "This is Frankie, Mom, Mrs. Stills," she said.

"He's a handsome one, honey. Looks like a keeper," said Mrs. Stills as she threw her mink wrap over her shoulder and took a drag off a cigarette in a holder.

"Pleased to make your acquaintance, ladies," said Frankie politely.

"Have a drink?" said Mrs. Stills.

"Don't mind if I do," said Frankie.

"Waiter, four martinis," she said to the waiter. "So what do you do, honey?" said Mrs. Stills.

"I'm a cabinetmaker," said Frankie.

"I got plenty of work to do on my building if you need any work. Plenty," she said as she gulped down her fourth martini. "I might be able to help you later, but right now, I'm busy, sorry," said Frankie. They finished their drinks and helped Mrs. Stills to the front of the hotel, where they put her in a cab and sent her home to Atherton. They walked down California to the apartment building, and Dhindi said, "Would you like to come in?"

"Yeah, sure," he said.

"So what do you do?" he asked.

"I work at a massage parlor on Taylor Street," she said once they were in the dull apartment she shared with her mother, who retired to her room. Dhindi, as free spirited and angelic as she was, managed this dingy building for the rich landlady and turned tricks at an all-night massage parlor in the Tenderloin, even though Frankie didn't care or really know what she was really doing.

"You are beautiful," he said as he stood up from where they were sitting, and he began kissing and caressing her. She was soft and feminine and melted into Frankie's embrace, kissing him passionately. He pulled her dress off and began licking her small breasts and continued down to her furry but fair bush and pulled down her panties. He got undressed, and they went into her bedroom and made love that really made bells ring and left the rest of the world behind. He would be seeing a lot more of Dhindi.

John was hanging around and happened to be attending City College of San Francisco. He was always talking about what great courses they had there and what great teachers were there, that Frankie should think about going. He was full of advice. Frankie still couldn't beat the motherfucker at chess.

Anna gathered her things and took off for Bolivia. Frankie rented out the room to a guy from Michigan—an average guy who, it turned out, had some good local connections, James.

Kim was around from time to time. Robert now had a piece of the Coop. Frankie and Malie hung around drinking beer and smoking pot some nights while they laughed and helped Robert with his sculpture and gave commentary, of course.

Glenda had a place at the corner of Fourteenth and Sanchez that Frankie would visit her at. He let her have the Caddy too.

Dhindi had a '68 MGB she didn't know how to drive, but Frankie did, and it was there. She didn't exactly tell him about her French boyfriend whom she had bought the car for (she was a real earner) who was in France and would be back someday.

But for now, the two of them would take trips up the coast or to the spots Frankie knew about near Union Valley, Jones Creek. Beautiful.

He was fulfilling his adolescent fantasy of having a beautiful brown-haired maiden wade naked at the end of the day in the alpine river that was calm and gold from the sunset while stoned on acid, of course. That particular camping trip was out of a Parrish painting. Night fell, and they gazed at each other and into the campfire then fell asleep in each other's arms.

During the joy and discovery of their new relationship, they decided to pay a visit to the new Mitchell Brothers Theater. They made pornography and were good pornographers. The first was *Behind the Green Door* with Marilyn Chambers, the Ivory Snow girl.

There was *Deep Throat* with Linda Lovelace. The broad could really suck some cock. After plunging her mouth over a twelve-inch cock and taking it all the way down her throat, she said, "I love it, I love it," with a big smile and then opened her mouth, sticking out her tongue and letting John Holmes shoot a load on her tongue. Turned out she recognized someone in one of the films and worked with her.

Unexpectedly Dhindi's French boyfriend showed up. He was a greasy little shit who went into a tirade when he found that Dhindi had been unfaithful and that Frankie was driving "his" car. Rather than kill the guy on the spot, Frankie threw him the keys to the car and said, "Here're the keys. Give me a ride home." They got in the car. Frankie really didn't fit in the back. Frenchy drove like a maniac down the bumpy cable car tracks running down California, so Frankie reached around and grabbed him by the throat and said, "Slow down!" Frenchy could see he better slow down and get this over with. She would show up again later, but for now it was her deception and her problem.

Panhandle Pete was at a party, and for some reason somebody hit him in the back of the head with a magnum of champagne.

Unconscious and bleeding from the ear, the emergency room doctors told those who brought him in that he would be fine, take a couple of aspirin and get some rest.

In the morning, Antonio found him on the floor in a pool of blood. He was rushed to the hospital and needless to say, all fucked up. He was paralyzed on half of his body, among other things. He was in the hospital for a while and recuperating at his place on Guerrero for a while until he was able to walk and function properly, with a limp. Good thing he had made plenty of money dealing acid, and didn't have to worry about making money.

Pete had the top floor of a beautiful Mediterranean building with built in stained glass, the great view of downtown. The type of place you see and say, "OooooHHHHH! I wonder who lives there," when you saw it.

Frankie found himself over there a lot watching the Watergate hearings. Pretty entertaining. That, of course, meant they were going to get the current administration. Get them. So they were applauding while Pete was convalescing.

"Eagle Krug is a bad dude. He'd never rat out his higher-ups like Dean and these other mama's boys who are singing like canaries," said Pete. He had already read everything there was to read about it, the *New York Times*, of course, and the underground rags who were the real ones to expose the truth about what happened. Frankie sat, and he watched and drew his own conclusions about what he saw and kept his mouth shut. To deviate from Pete's take on things was to invite trouble, so he watched and listened.

He hadn't called Mimi for a while. He knew that taking time allowed her to get more comfortable with him. She had just graduated Berkeley High, her mother was a head—it was very chaotic to grow up in such an environment then. She also had some possessive boyfriend who wouldn't just leave her alone. Frankie had to give her shelter. *Relax, it's going to be okay.* "Mimi, hi, it's Frankie. How ya doing dear?"

"Oh, I'm fine, good to hear from you."

"What do you think about coming to the City and going dancing Saturday night?"

"Yeah, I'd love to," she said. "If you want to come a little earlier, we could have dinner in North Beach."

"What time?"

"My place at six."

"Okay, I'll be there." Six o'clock, Saturday, the doorbell rang. "Hi, how are you? Oh, you look great."

"Hi," she said shyly. She was tall, blond, healthy, of German descent, and smoking hot. Nice body, dance, oh yeah.

"You have a car, right?"

"Yeah, wanna drive?" She held up the keys.

"I'll drive." They had a nice dinner at Enrico's and walked down the street the new hottest nightclub in North Beach, the Carousel Ballroom, formerly the Big Basket.

It was an early disco that no particular group owned. It was half gay, half hetero types, everybody. It wasn't too crowded (ah, the good old days), plenty of room to dance, and dance they did. Frankie had the steps from his days of bumping and grinding with Miss Thing, and Mimi was a student of modern, jazz, and ballet and had moves. They danced and danced and drank some gin and tonics until the music stopped. They had burned off the nervous energy and now wanted to strip off their clothes and make love like animals until the sun came up.

Frankie was in the living room one day watching sports and began looking at the film sitting there, where it had been for months. He took one out of the foiled Kodak paper wrappers and took a closer look. He could see that it had been taken apart and put back together, but not in a factory. He pulled off one side of the film canister and looked at it. It was coke.

In the eight-millimeter canisters were fourteen ounces of coke. He turned John on to some, then James, the roommate, and everybody else who wanted some. Soon the entire neighborhood was hanging around, doing lines, listening to music, playing chess.

"I know someone who will buy everything you got," said James.

Frankie really didn't know anything about the guy even though they lived together. "Oh yeah, how much you think I can get for this?" asked Frankie.

"About eleven hundred dollars an ounce," he said. He seemed to know what he was talking about. He thought back to the time in Cambridge when he set up a deal with friends of Ronnie's (black guys) and a pot dealer from the local natural food restaurant, also a friend of Ronnie's. They had them drive them to the deepest, darkest Roxbury (Boston's black ghetto) and gave them the pot, and they went into the house and didn't come out. There was no way two white boys were going to go into that house and get that pot. They were so stupid and got ripped off. "I thought you said they were friends of Ronnie's?" asked the natural food guy.

"They were!" said Frankie.

"Okay, set it up."

"I'll give them ten ounces for eleven thousand dollars," said Frankie.

"Okay," said James. "It's totally uncut, so they should be happy with that." He was saying all the right things.

"I will come along. It's not leaving my possession until I have the cash in my hand," said Frankie.

"No problem, these people are very cool," said James. They went to a warehouse South of Market, down a dark alley. Out from the inner sanctum came a guy to take a sample to be tested for purity. He scooped a small amount out of the big baggie full of the white powder and went back into the inner sanctum through a door in a larger roll-up door. A few minutes passed, and the guy came through the door again holding a stack of money and put it on the table where the bag of coke sat, picked up the bag, stuck out his hand to shake, and said, "Nice doing business with you."

Frankie shook the guy's hand and said, "Glad you're happy." Frankie had his eye on a '57 Jaguar XK140 for sale at a lot owned by a couple of young guys on Army Street. He now had the $1,400 they wanted for it and hurried on down to make the purchase.

Frankie had been hanging around with a gay hairdresser named Lee. He was young, tall, and very stylish. He knew every hot chick in town and probably cut their hair. He was very good at that. Lee also liked Qualudes and was usually half awake and slurring but still rather attractive. Frankie liked going out with him, his new Jag, a pocket full of coke. They hit the town.

After a night of dancing, drinking, and snorting coke in North Beach, heading up Army Street, and going through the Guerrero intersection, some dumb kid turned left right in front of the Jag. Frankie really couldn't believe the kid was so stupid. He had to have it towed to Arroyo Brother's body shop on the corner of Seventeenth and Valencia, next to the Coop. He was done with the Coop. Richard drank so much he would have attacks where he would roll around on the floor and gyrate uncontrollably. Frankie was tired of this and felt Richard was just seeking attention because everyone would come to his aid and walk him around and give him another drink to make him feel better. After his fairly long tenure there and all the good times he had in the back hanging out with Robert and Malie, Frankie got in a scuffle with Richard (who was totally out of control anyway) and got in a verbal exchange with Bobby, a goofy-looking little fag who did the books and was the only person on earth who would have sucked Richard's dusty cock. "You little cunt!" Frankie told him. Bobby was the only person who could stomach the office where Richard lived and barfed in the waste basket on a regular basis. He would still go in and see what Robert was up to and stay friends with Malie and sell him his "shit."

Frankie bought a bunch of new clothes, a new stereo, a bunch of stuff. He sent Glenda out on shopping sprees and Mimi over for nights out on the town. He was able to squire Glenda and Mimi around together. They handled it well. It was something Frankie could get used to, but it was Mimi he wanted as his new old lady.

Lee worshipped David Bowie and played *Diamond Dogs* constantly. He hung out on the *Dogs* tour and knew what the songs were all about. One afternoon, he was over and got Frankie lying on his bed and began sucking his cock. He was a big tall Oklahoman with a big hard dick which he stuck in Frankie's face, expecting him to suck it. Lee didn't realize Frankie wasn't gay but figured it out when Frankie hopped up and said, "I can't do this."

With the Jag finally fixed, Frankie planned a long trip with Glenda up to a lake where Betty was camping with her mother (Frankie's real grandmother), whom Frankie had always known as Aunt Casey. During the Depression, Casey gave Betty to her older brother, Ole, and his wife, Hazel, who were hardworking and had the means to raise the child. Frankie always thought Ole and Hazel were his grandparents and fit the role for him. Only when she was eighteen did they tell her the truth. She didn't take it too well. Ole died from a hard life of working from dawn to dusk as a farmer, and Hazel remarried. Betty didn't like Mike, whom Betty said beat horses. None of this was explained. Betty just disowned Hazel, and when Casey reemerged, she was the grandma, but she really wasn't. She was Aunt Casey; she apparently had a checkered past no one wanted to talk about. Frankie didn't care except that Hazel still considered Frankie a grandson, and she was more than a great aunt to him. Betty was fucked up.

Casey and her husband, Andy, loved to camp and fish, and Betty was with them.

Frankie and Glenda met up with the next day and from there decided to drive to Oregon and take Dana with them and visit some relatives.

It was summertime and hot. The Jag ran cooler at 120 miles per hour than at 80, so Frankie went 120 miles per hour. Ahead was a gray dot on the road. It was an official state vehicle with a geeky state worker going about forty-five. He looked in the rearview mirror to make sure there was no traffic coming and changed into the fast lane to pass an even slower going truck. Upon his move into the fast lane, he looked in the rearview mirror to see a red Jaguar and three long-haired freaks a couple of feet behind him, filling his mirror. They could see the guy jump. He must have called the Oregon Highway Patrol. They put out speed traps behind the fast-moving trio, who finally stopped at a gas station to cool off and have a drink. Sitting in the shade, they saw a cop in a big hurry to get to the freeway until he spotted them and parked in sight of them, ready to pounce the moment they began moving. Frankie decided to outwait the cop, and he finally departed, defeated.

They continued on up to northern Oregon and stopped in The Dalles. They drew a lot of attention, so it was their good fortune that their Uncle Marvin was a cop in the sleepy town. He somehow intercepted them and escorted them to their modest home in town, which looked like Mayberry.

"Uncle Marvin, good to see you. How are you? It's been a long time," said Frankie as he got out of the car.

"Look at you. You're all grown up. And, Dana, look at that hair," said Uncle Marv, not in an approving way, but he was smiling nevertheless. "This is Glenda, my girlfriend," he said and introduced them.

"You look hot. Come on in," he said. "How about some lemonade?' Innie," he called out when they entered the house.

Innie emerged from the back bedroom. "Frankie, Dana, oh look at you," she said very lovingly and came quickly to hug and give them pecks on the cheeks. "Come in and cool off in front of the air conditioner. You look hot. Frankie introduced Glenda. "What kind of car is that, honey?"

"It's a Jaguar. British," he said.

"Never seen one of those before," she said.

"Looks fast. What's under the hood?" asked Marv.

"An inline 6, dual overhead cam, three carburetors," said Frankie. They stayed the night and shoved off in the morning, saying their goodbyes. The three went to Hood River, where Frankie was born, in view of the year-round snowcapped Mount Hood. The valley was orchards, fields, ranches. They drove by Grandfather Ole's apple orchard where Betty grew up and went for a swim in the river. It was a simple, wholesome life that people in the region lived. Frankie took it in and was headed in a different direction. Time to take some acid. Glenda didn't take any because she was still bleeding from the abortion she got before they left. Sitting between Frankie and Dana on the console, bumping along at high rates of speed, could not have helped her condition.

The trio traveled at night with the stereo blasting "Born to be Wild," doing at least a hundred miles per hour. The rear of the car started waving back and forth. The tire was fine, but the aging wire wheeled rim had broken off the hub except for two spokes. Close one, could have been disastrous. Good thing there was a good spare. They'd have been stuck in the middle of nowhere.

They deposited Dana in Sacramento and returned to the City. Glenda was fine, but it was sad they didn't live together anymore in the domestic bliss they had once known.

He was anxious to get into what was left of the almost quarter pound of coke he had. And he did, went on a three-day binge. He didn't stop to think about whether it was a good idea to snort his brains out and turn himself into a babbling idiot. Then he started seeing bugs in the coke. He was delirious, but he thought it was fine. *Do another line, Frankie.* He came down, caught some sleep, cleaned himself up, ate, and gave Mimi a call. "Hello, dear. Frankie. Wanna come over?"

"Yeah, when?"

"Right now," he said. She came over, and they had a lovely evening, which after dinner, they had a little coke to make the time they had to fuck like a couple of beautiful horny young adults. They may have been twenty and eighteen respectively, but they were smart and knew what was going on.

The one thing they didn't do was question the direction it was all going. The hatred was directed to Tricky Dick, and there was no choice other than go along with the People's Park crowd that were all about overthrowing the government and starting over. The entire educational system and government in charge had to be overthrown, if you were hip.

"What do you say we take a ride down the coast," said Frankie.

"Sounds fun," she said. They had a pleasant ride down Highway 1 to Carmel and beyond. South before the Bixby Bridge where the Carmel River flowed into the ocean was Palo Colorado Canyon and Garrapata. On his twentieth birthday, he was depressed (getting old), so he drove the MGB down that way; took acid, of course; and picked up a hitchhiker named Rocko, who showed him around and lived in a teepee up in the hills. From Highway 1, he turned left and drove through a eucalyptus grove right before the bridge, up the hill, to a settled area near a small river at the bottom of the canyon. There were huge coastal redwoods in a verdant dark-green environment with ferns and the sound of water gently falling. The road climbed out into drier foothills, oak trees, mansanita, and pine trees. It climbed back into a coastal pine environment at the end of about a ten-mile road. Truly one of the most beautiful places on earth.

They came down from wonderland (also known as Dogpatch by the hippies who lived in Garrapata) and parked. They went for a walk down a trail by the bridge down to the beach.

They were stoned on acid, and Frankie could see she was vulnerable even though she was a strong girl. He felt protective of her. This was the first trip the two of them would make. They took the same trip later in Mimi's Camaro, and it was raining cats and dogs. Like a dumbass, Frankie decided to try to negotiate the mud road going up to Rocko's teepee. He got a hundred yards up the road and realized he wasn't going to make it. He parked it and watched a VW bug with a few longhairs in it go bombing by up the muddy road at a high rate of speed, with no problem. Frankie and Mimi walked in the pouring rain up the hill looking for Rocko, following the long road up the remote canyon ridge. For quite a while, they walked. No Rocko. But down the road, in the mud, came a merry hippie fellow. "Hi, how ya doing?" he said.

"Good, we're looking for a guy named Rocko. Do you know him?" asked Frankie.

"No, I don't. Is there a problem?" he said.

"Our car is stuck, and we'd like to call a tow truck," said Frankie.

"You won't find a phone up here. Let's take a look at your car," said the nice fellow. "I'm Dulcimer Seed, I make dulcimers."

"Frankie and Mimi. The car is a mile or so down this road," said Frankie. "You live here?" he asked.

"Yeah, a couple of miles down the road, by the river," he said. The sun came out and revealed the true beauty of the place. Other than being wet and cold, they were happy to be there, stoned on acid. They got to the car. Dulcimer Seed looked at Frankie and said, "You can't drive that out of here?"

"No, I didn't want it to slide into the hill and damage the side," said Frankie. The car was not getting traction and was sliding sideways instead of forward, and to the side was a mud and rock embankment that the car was about to slide into.

He hopped in the car and did exactly what Frankie was afraid he'd do. Now the car was stuck in the mud with the driver's side door was against the rock and mud wall. "Yeah, I see what you mean," he said as he climbed out of the passenger side door. "Let's go call a tow truck," he said. They were too stoned and wet, as the rain started to fall again, to be pissed off. They just wanted to get the car and go home.

They finally got to a neighbor's house to call the tow truck. Dulcimer Seed then came out and said, "Okay, they'll be here in an hour. My place is right over there," he said. He lived in a wonderful mountain cabin. He started a fire and gave them some tea and something to eat. Lights shone in the window "Tow truck's here."

"Goodbye, thank you," he said as they left and got into the tow truck. It had been raining and raining, and the road was a mud river. The tow truck driver was none too happy about almost getting his truck stuck at night in the rain in the middle of nowhere, rescuing couple of stoned kids too stupid to know not to drive on such a road in the rain.

He dragged the Camaro down the hill (scratching the side of the car) in a controlled slide until they were back on pavement.

Frankie spent the afternoons at Pete's watching the Watergate hearings. It was civics for radical, antiestablishment acid heads. Frankie watched and listened. It was also important time in American history. John Dean, with his hot wife nobly sitting behind him during his testimony, would spill the beans. Nixon was fucked, and the entertainment value of watching it happen was worth watching.

John finally talked Frankie into taking a look at classes offered at City College, and he was ready to go once he saw all the stuff he wanted to know about being offered. He just had to get some money, so he applied for grants and loans and got them. Frankie had already gotten his GED when he was on Hermann Street, so he was going to college, far out. He took genetics, astronomy (at 7:00 a.m.), Change in America Society (early interdisciplinary brainwashing, to radicalize the student body), jewelry making, Chinese brush painting, and gymnastics, a full load.

He was, of course, still doing coke at all hours of the day and night and staying up a lot. He was invincible; he could handle it.

Dhindi was no longer in the picture, but she did leave Frankie with two ringneck doves that cooed in the mornings and throughout the day. She had no place to keep them, so Frankie turned Michelle's room into an aviary. He built a large cage in a large portion of the room from ceiling to floor and dedicated the rest of the room to a greenhouse with dozens of plants, with the morning sun beaming in. Frankie knew he had stayed up too late when the birds would go off at dusk; he would have to go into the dark attic to get as far away from them as he could to get any sleep. He would be starting school so would have to start getting up with them.

But the all-night partying just kept up. John and Frankie played chess, Frankie never won, and the attic was more and more the place to hang out and shoot his bow and arrow at the target he dragged up there. Then there was lighting then music, and the world outside just got further and further away. Time was not so relevant in the attic; you could do what you wanted. Frankie had plenty of friendly nostrils hanging around helping him too.

He also used the attic to weigh grams, eighths, and whatever other measurement of coke his growing clientele requested. He was now in business, the drug business.

Frankie got his shit together and made it to the first day of school. Astronomy was in the observatory, on the fourth floor of the main building, at 7:00 a.m. It would be a difficult class to make, especially after an all-nighter when alcohol was consumed in large quantities. That would be Mondays, Wednesdays, Fridays. Then genetics, with a very popular and interesting professor who had been there since World War II. Frankie would develop a close relationship with this very brilliant man, and he was greatly influenced by him in the two semesters to come. Tuesdays and Thursdays, it was gymnastics, which he loved and was good at but was too tall for competition. The hot blonde teacher was always trying to get Frankie involved in extracurricular activities. Not sex or anything, but dance and theatrical performances. He said he would but never made it due to the fact he was getting fucked up with his friends or banging some hot little slut when he should be doing his homework. There would be no all-nighters before that early class where he was working on parallel bars and rings. Then there was jewelry class. He had a great teacher who saw his potential and cut him loose. He aided him in executing his designs for rings and bracelets he already had in his head, and out of this class would come some great pieces. Change in American society was heavily accredited class with three teachers each from different areas of study. They were all very liberal. The students were required to read a book a week, write a report on it, and give a presentation on the book. It was five hours a week, five units.

Frankie realized why John talked him into going there—so he had someone to argue with. John was a philosophy and political science major and on his way to UC Berkeley.

Robert and Adrianna moved from their crummy little house in Brisbane to another crummy little house in Brisbane. But this crummy little house was on a very large lot, up from the school, and had a full-sized mother in law in the back, which Robert turned into a studio. There was a huge oak tree where Robert hung a ship's hatch cover that swung over a large area with a barbeque pit and dining area. It had a tetherball court, with a pole and ball, a boccie ball (on uneven terrain), court, and a fish pond that didn't hold water. Many a drunken tetherball, boccie ball matches. Tough John was often around for a rough and tumble game of boccie ball. Adrianna was usually putting together a barbeque. Frankie got away from the City and hung out there quite a bit, after his studies, of course.

Frankie's brother Dana was there one weekend, and he took him to Brisbane for a little acid in the afternoon. "This can't be the acid I gave you a year ago," he said to Robert when he showed him the blotter.

"Okay, whatever you say. That's it, though. Here's two for you and Dana, and I'll take these two," Frankie said to Robert as he popped five hundred mics of some very strong acid into his mouth. Maybe he was showing off, or maybe he was just stupid, but Robert looked deep into his eyes with a knowing smile and put on Rick Wakeman's *Journey to the Center of the Earth* and went into the back yard with Dana. Frankie was hanging on to his tongue for about five hours while taking the scary and bumpy journey to the earth's core and back.

Robert and Dana came in later and looked at him through fish eye lens and talked to each other as if Frankie wasn't there.

"You okay? Frankie, you all right?" Robert leaned in and asked.

"Fine, fine, you?" he said automatically.

"He's okay," said Robert.

It would be the first time in his life he was too fucked up (on acid) to drive. Being stoned on acid made one a much better driver, if you didn't get pulled over for going five miles per hour. Dana wasn't too stoned; he was happy to drive the Jag.

Frankie was turning twenty-one, and he planned a party. Glenda was there, and Adrianna was there, providing food. Malie and his wife, Lillie, a large Samoan woman always laughing at everybody and everything, came. Lillie was probably tougher than everybody there, including her husband, Malie (shark, the toughest motherfucker). Samoan women were tougher than the men. Panhandle Pete, Antonio, some of the boys from the Coop, Robert, some neighbors, Michelle's ex-boyfriend Billy, and his new girlfriend (a psycho who drove her hot rod Citron, if there was such a thing, at high rates of speed on 101 from Mill Valley through the tunnel and to the Golden Gate) were there. Her sister Cybil, the one with nice cans, and Naomi, their hot girlfriend were also there. Malisol, a Lebanese-looking babe; her sister, who was a trapeze star; and Kim, of course, and his crowd were there as well. Frankie wished he had a trapeze set up. Lee and some slit-eyed fags—not that they were Asian or anything, they were just fucked up, like on Quaaludes—also went. Word got out that there were free drugs, and people flocked from miles around.

Gordon was such a great friend. He gave Frankie the pyramid he made. It was made from a bunch of small oak blocks. It was 12×12 inches with a hidden drawer in the middle where the king's chamber was with a track and a drawer slide with one row at the bottom of the drawer in the center. He hung a central row with free-hanging blocks (with the magnets in it) that would have to be aligned with due north to open. Genius.

Unfortunately, Frankie invited a dope from the Coop who couldn't hold his liquor and who brought his out-of-control four-year-old who was unattended and broke a fragile antique parquet cigarette dispenser that someone gave Frankie as a present. He had to ask him to leave, and in a fit, he scooped up his daughter and stormed out. The guy was a dick.

But that was the worst of it. Coke was being snorted upstairs, in the attic; the not so familiar were downstairs eating, drinking, and dancing until the cops showed up and told them to turn it down.

He wore his beautiful beige snakeskin shoes, white fitted pleated slacks, and peach floral fitted shirt (from Jizz). Every broad there wanted to fuck him. He was at the top of his game; it was the highlight of his career.

He was a serious student to prove he could do it and if anything used coke to assist him in his studies, sometimes all night long to write a paper. He toiled with the problems presented to him regarding Genetics and Change in American Society. The coke was running out, but he developed a market for it and realized it couldn't end.

From jewelry class, he met a hipster, Michael. He was also a friend of John's. A Vietnam veteran with long blond hair and an army issue coat from Wyoming, he had an infectious laugh, played chess, and snorted coke. He lived in a dive with a bunch of French assholes on Market Street between Church and Sanchez. His ex old lady was French.

The three of them would have chess playing tournaments. Frankie could beat Michael, who could beat John, but Frankie still couldn't beat John. Weird.

Frankie asked Mimi to move in with him, and she said yes. It was kind of painful because Glenda still had stuff there, and she was realizing she was out and Mimi was in.

It got Mimi out of her mother's house, which was dysfunctional and a source of neurosis, and filled their needs to cut loose and have crazy sex, which they did.

They set up house, but there was no need to rush things. Mimi was interested in attending the city college herself, and with encouragement from John, she enrolled. A fresh new vibe inhabited the house, and in the true sense of the word, she brought a beautiful presence to the place.

It was notable that when the cute girls at the city college noticed Frankie and his cool car, they wanted a ride somewhere. "I have a girlfriend, but never mind that. Where can I take you?" he'd say. He never did get laid, but who had time for that anyway? He was busy.

Frankie had a growing business selling small amounts of pot, coke, and acid. He had been in hand enough in the recent past to generate a group of people, through word of mouth, who wanted the kind of drugs Frankie had. He had burned through what he had with nothing to show for it and had to sell the Jag or get a job.

Across the street at Church Street was a store that had very cool, unusual hanging ferns, outrageous stained-glass lamps with amber and semiprecious stones inset, as well as arts and crafts—Plain Dealing. Bobby and Anabelle, from New Orleans, were their neighbors, whom Frankie, John, and Mimi became friends with. They had great taste and some high-powered friends from that part of the world. Not only did they have the storefront but lived upstairs in the beautiful Victorian, with the best of the hanging ferns and stained glass. Bear Owsly was a friend of theirs. Bobby was from New Orleans and connected. Jack Casady (although from DC) from the Jefferson Airplane was among their friends from Louisiana.

Frankie was still keeping an eye on the Watergate saga and saw Panhandle Pete from time to time. One of Pete's attributes was introducing people he knew to one another whom he knew would become friends; he networked. To his credit, he never really asked anything for it either. It was not uncommon for the person who put the connections together to ask for a cut or "piece of the action," which, after all, was what dealing drugs was—getting it from those who had them and getting them to the people that wanted them and making a lot of money. Those he introduced to one another definitely did deals and made money.

Pete introduced Frankie and Mimi to Karen and Carlos, who lived on Union Street, top of Nob Hill. The Hog Farm bus was parked out front with the clan living in it, visiting, and camping out. Carlos was a streetwise native of the City who'd already gotten over a heroin addiction and was having a kid with his beloved Karen. He was now foreman of a woodshop for a waterbed company and a very good woodworker, having built a dining room table and other furniture for their happy, hip home. He was also Vicki's ex old man, so Frankie heard lots of stories about how bad he had it (the heroin addiction) but made a lot of money dealing and always managed to keep his shit together. They hit it troff and became good friends, and Carlos was a good connection.

He sold the Jag but had the '59 Caddy, which he drove to Oakdale to visit Patrice. They, by then, had a lifetime of different experiences, but it was fun to see her and her kid. He didn't do the math, but the kid didn't look anything like Frankie. She was just the kind of girl who would not tell the dad if it was the case, he thought later. She was resourceful and perfectly capable of raising a kid on her own. He gave it to her for old time's sake and bid her a farewell. "Come visit me in the City," he said. She did, at a most unexpected time. It was not a problem; he was just having an all-nighter with a bunch of people. "Here, do a line," he said.

At school, he became engaged and found his voice especially when it came to race and equality. He knew about civil rights and how the black man was held down for so long. He knew it was not that long ago that full equality had not been given to negros everywhere, especially in the South. What he didn't understand was why the black man had not taken advantage of his freedom and opportunities. The cultural revolution—black people were in the midst of the equality they had won. There were too many angry black people (especially in the Change in American Society class) who just went on and on about whitey, and they just couldn't let it go. They were mad.

He was white—guilty by race. Not much he could do about that. They treated him like shit, and he didn't like that. He was a tough street kid and didn't get intimidated by spoiled black assholes talking shit. He was not prejudiced and couldn't understand why they were. Didn't do them any good except guilt white liberals and make everyone keep their mouths shut.

The guys on Army Street had a nice '62 MGA that Frankie had to have, $500. He had to juggle some sources of income (student loan was on the way) to make the purchase. It wasn't as fast as Robert's TR3 but cornered better, which made up for the difference in engine displacement, 2,000 cc to the 1,600 cc the MG had.

Bobby came over one day with a big bag of pot and said, "See what you can do with this. It's real fresh, beautiful Mexican. About two hundred fifty a pound, here's five."

"I'll see what I can do," he said. He moved about fifty pounds to his backup coke dealer in Oakland, Mad Dog, for $350.

He moved pounds to Billy, in Marin, with the looney girlfriend. Now a good source of coke as well. Donny, Anna's former boyfriend and owner of the Good Karma, bought some. Frankie fronted Chet some and got paid eventually. It was good weed, and the price was right.

It also fulfilled a social need for someone like Frankie, as sometimes what dealing and doing drugs does for people. People wanted to talk to you, wheeling and dealing were going on; you were in demand, the focus of attention, and had drugs, which everybody wanted.

It was also a delicate act to manage. Since it was illegal, you could not afford to piss anybody off but had to get paid without having to get rough or anything like that. So it was a political position you as a dealer would have to assume as well as one of a diplomat.

Frankie and Mimi had their own rooms but mostly slept in Frankie's bed. Nothing happened to set off fireworks yet. They were still getting used to the arrangement. Mimi was still pretty young and not necessarily empty-headed but did not possess great social skills. No wonder, there wasn't really a handbook.

It's actually what he liked about Malie. They were content to just hang out. No talking. They were hanging out; why clutter it up with words? They hung out and were quiet, and say what? It was about this time that Dak showed up. He liked coke too, and having been busted and spent two years in Santa Rita, he was not the rich acid dealer he had once been. He had been a good friend to Frankie in the past, and at least Frankie could do was to help Dak out and let him stay in the attic for a while. He moved a bunch of shit up there and made it livable for a while. He wasn't around a lot. It wasn't long before fate called him back to Berkeley, and he moved out, leaving behind a great space.

School was interesting, but Frankie realized he had bitten off more than he could chew. The load was just too much of a burden. He did fine and got mostly Bs, but competing with John, who got As, was just too much. Frankie took a couple of required courses (Health, English, and Reading—a great class, How to Read a Book) the next semester. He stayed with Gymnastics, Jewelry, and Cultural Anthropology, which he really liked. Mimi was going and took entirely different classes, except jewelry making. City College was like a big high school, so it was like filling a void that Frankie had, having left in his sophomore year in high school.

The year 1973, Marvin Gaye, Al Green, and Curtis Mayfield made great R&B. Bowie, Pink Floyd, and Frank Zappa (Hot Rats) caught Frankie's attention. Frankie theorized that with the introduction of coke, a lot of musicians were peeking out from behind some curtain somewhere. It turned out to be addictive, didn't matter whether it was physical or psychological. It started out as a social drug but for most became an addiction. Oh, it was a disease. Bullshit. Didn't matter.

It led many to withdraw, hide. Hide away so they could do more drugs, and they were too fucked up to get back to doing what you were doing prior.

The attic became not only an archery range, an office for weighing drugs, a model building work area (Frankie in his spare time built models of cars, something he did as a kid) Nazi highway patrol and that sort of thing, but it also became someplace to hide.

While being a place to hide out and do more drugs, it was the perfect place to have crazy sex. He set up a Japanese love swing, silk ropes for tying nasty girls up while fucking them. Mimi, once out of her shell, participated wholeheartedly in the kinky fun. Being of German descent had to have something to do with it. They were into more than just plain sex; it was theater. Like Mick Jagger said, "All the perverts never have to worry about time passing by."

Having grown up in the City, John knew a lot of people, some of whom were into selling drugs. He introduced Frankie to Dave Landry. He lived in a rundown Victorian on Post and Webster. They did a fair amount of business when Frankie couldn't find what he needed anywhere else. Dave did not have the best-quality shit; he cut it too much. He had a ditsy girlfriend, and her sister lived with them. John invited them along with Frankie and Mimi to his parents' schoolhouse in Navarro, in Anderson Valley, between Boonville and Mendicino. John's girlfriend, Judy, top ballet dancer and teacher at Dance Spectrum and formerly the S. F. Ballet, came along.

It was built in 1850 by the original Scottish and Irish settlers who came to Anderson Valley to grow fruits and vegetables for their children to receive a traditional education. It was a beautiful building with two very large classrooms. The back classroom was so big they turned it into a Badminton/Volleyball court for recreation and lots of fun, and the front classroom was a kitchen/bathroom with a woodburning stove with a dozen or so overstuffed chairs around it with a library of hundreds of books to read. It was good to get out of the City, do some swimming in the river (and other great places very remote and only known to locals), play a little badminton, and read a book.

They were growing up. Mimi was probably more mature than Frankie, even though she was younger than him. She was the oldest kid in the family, and with mom either drinking or smoking pot all day long, the role of taking care of her younger brothers and sisters fell to her. Their domestic life was a success. Mimi was not the least bit combative. If Frankie got mad, she looked at him with loving, innocent eyes and without a word would make him feel like the fool that he was to ever get angry and shut him off like a switch. Her very nature canceled out getting into a back-and-forth type of fight most fools in love on the planet engage in.

They took a trip to the Sierras and picked up brother Dana on their way through Sacramento. They took acid with little brother at the highest lake in Crystal Basin, above Union Valley, Icehouse, and Jones Creek. Frankie chugged some grapefruit juice before the acid. He couldn't believe that he never knew to never drink citrus before taking acid. He learned the hard way. He was hurting.

The highest lake (reservoir actually) at the top of the mountain range was Loon Lake. He had never been there but was curious about it. It had been worked and not in a good way; in fact it was kind of tortured, probably by the Department of Water Resources or Army Corps of Engineers or some government agency at the time that had no regard for the way any of it looked, and it was not pretty. It was still an amazing place. Top of the world.

It had a peninsula jutting out into the lake, and it was actually floating. Whatever kind of heavy equipment they had in there to create a reservoir had also made a bizarre land configuration that made three stoned kids wonder about what they were seeing.

If one stood up on the top of the range and looked west, they could smell the ocean in the stiff wind blowing through them, cold and biting, from the Pacific Ocean. If one walked down to the water on the east side of the landmass, wayward, it was hot and the air was thin, without a hint of wind. It was three feet above their heads; one had to take off their shirt.

Trying to be grasshopper, Dana asked, "What is Zen?" while they were sitting on the rocks looking into Loon Lake. Mimi had already figured out the climate and was sitting on a rock with her shoes off and feet in the water, hands folded, looking to see what "Mr. Know-It-All" was going to answer. Mr. Know-It-All pointed to her and said, "That's Zen." At least he knew that.

Mimi was a saint, but it must have been by chance because her family was a mess. There was Cybil (yes, nice cans), Jenny (also nice cans), Lute (a younger brother not wanting to have anything to do with the crazy faction of the family, which was everybody), and Nana (half black from a traveling black guy, never seen or heard from again). His claim to fame was that he was Maya Angelou's brother. Mom, Marguirette, was an artist from a wealthy Pennsylvanian family; she never worked a day in her life and was an alcoholic, drug addict. Marguirette had her problems but was a loving and talented woman whom Frankie grew to love, even though Mimi hid her eyes when it came to talking about her mother. She had dough, and even though it made her a different person than those who had to work for a living, she was generous and always laughing. She was a gas. When Frankie met her, she had a biker boyfriend, Jack, a Hells Angel.

Cybil was overcome by a clown Frankie knew from North Beach Leather and had moved up to his own North Beach Leather store on Telegraph, Mark. Mark was from New York and really liked coke. He had moved right in to Marguirette's Berkeley Hills house with his dick hard, chasing Cybil around, trying to pin the tail on the donkey. They had the downstairs, which meant it was off limits to the rest of the family. Mark had connections. Frankie and he would do a little business, but it was usually such a hassle. Frankie tried to avoid the guy.

The family moved to Cupertino so Arnie could work with his good buddy Raz at Bechtel building BART. Frankie zipped down there to visit to see the fancy new house with a pool and got the hell out, back to the City. It was a nice visit, quick.

In 1974, Nixon refused to turn over the tapes. Dumb shows like *The Six Million Dollar Man* hit the little screen, *Monty Python's Flying Circus* (Robert's favorite show) ended production, the Jefferson Starship came into being, the Ramons played their first show at CBGB, Nixon resigned, Ford pardoned Nixon, and Patty Hearst was kidnapped by the Symbionese Liberation Army. Far out.

Glenda moved up in the world and got a place near the Wharf, on Bay Street, a nice place. He would go see her occasionally, have dinner, and hang out with Gary and Julius. There was still a connection there. She knew he went to Sacramento from time to time. Arnie, for reasons unknown to Frankie, left his BART job and went back to Sacramento and got his old job back at the state. Glenda needed a car and knew the place to buy one was Sacramento. She gave him $1,400 cash to have him buy her one. She had taken up smuggling for Gary and had some dough. She could look very straight and taped hash to her stomach on flights from South America.

He enlisted Arnie to help him buy the car for Glenda on the visit he and Mimi made that summer. Arnie liked Mimi all right, but he really liked Glenda, and when given the challenge of getting Glenda a good deal, he almost beat up the poor used car salesman. He hated used car salesmen. Frankie found a beautiful '66 Dodge Polara in mint condition for $1,400. Arnie made sure that it was not a penny more. They didn't know what they had.

Mimi followed closely in her Camaro back to the City. Glenda loved the car; it was a real score.

Mimi's father had been divorced from Marguirette at least six or seven years before then. Frankie could not imagine them ever having been married, let alone have had a bunch of kids when he met him. Don was a very large man, probably six feet, six inches, and had remarried. His wife was a psychiatric nurse named Victoria. They invited Frankie and Mimi over for dinner to their house in the Berkeley Hills that he designed and built. He was an architect.

Frankie was not impressed. It was early Minimalist. Could have been a cafeteria or a hospital. His wife was dangerous, a very scary person, just because she held disturbing views about how to treat people with psychological and psychiatric disorders. Don was a big marshmallow of a man, a man of no will. His crazy wife had him wrapped around her finger. Marguirette had a story about him when she said she punched him in the stomach and he put his hand on it and said, "Aaawwwwhhhh."

Chet had a place a couple of blocks away on Twenty-Fourth and Noe. Like a mother-in-law, in the middle of the block with his German shepherd, Foot, he drove a full-sized International truck that was full of shit, windows never washed—kind of like his glasses.

He came by from time to time with the best weed. Real Gold Colombian and real Red Colombian, simply outstanding at the time. Frankie always bought whatever he had. He did have the best connections.

At the time, he had a massage table and was into physical therapeutics. He was always rolling his head around, looking up as if to be releasing tension or something.

Down the street from them on Church was a half Mexican, half Filipino, he said. Bernardo was his name. They called him BBQ. He was a crazy local kid who didn't make English class.

He did make it to gym, though, and was a pretty good athlete. Though not well educated, he did have a lot of good stories, which he told with his big fat fingers sticking straight out as he talked about whose ass he was going to kick. He would take Frankie up to Day Street Gym to play basketball with "The Smith Cough Drop Brothers" and "Corn-smelling, Nappy-Headed Niggers." Dave Casper, from the Raiders, would show up to play sometimes. Also, Hondo Hamer, who lived across the street from the gym, came to play. He and his brothers were of Hawaiian descent. Hondo was as wide as he was tall. "That porky can move," BBQ would say. He beat Frankie at racquetball, and Frankie was good. That porky could move.

A character from up yonder Navarro way, a friend, or at least an acquaintance, of John's, Pogo came around and liked smoking pot and snorting coke. He wanted to get right in the middle of it. He was actually very bright, read a lot, and was a country boy. He had been a lumberjack not that long ago.

Frankie still ate at the Good Karma Cafe now and again. Donnie, the owner, was realizing the benefits of good food and good health but also not dipping your nose into the bag when selling cocaine. Sell it to dumbasses like Frankie and his friends, who were. There was a constant parade of fools wanting to get stupid, or stupider, with the help of cocaine. They could talk like crazy, make no sense, and talk even more. Blah, blah, blah, they loved to hear themselves talk that make no sense. It didn't matter whether they made any sense or not. It was a real yakfest; they stayed up for days talking about, well, they'll never know, but it seemed meaningful at the time. There was a contingent that thought it made you smarter, more insightful. Not.

Frankie and Mimi made trips up Highway 1 in the MGA and found places of great beauty to pull off and have relations, sexual relations, in the bushes, in the weeds. Frankie was very satisfied with the relationship.

Malie and Lily moved a block away to a place on Duncan and Dolores (to be close to Frankie) and came by every Friday after work to get his shit. It was a ritual that worked like clockwork. He was always home at that time. Malie was an important friend, not to mention the toughest Samoan around, no doubt.

He told a story of going into a Mexican bar where some Samoans had gotten into a fight a few days earlier. He was by himself, and in the bathroom, he was approached by a Mexican wielding a gun. The Mexican backed him into a corner and fired a couple of shots, which ricocheted off the walls. He grabbed the guy, took the gun away, and "beat him on the floor until he didn't wake up." He killed the guy and was arrested but later released when the fact it was self-defense became clear.

On the same block of Dolores Street that Malie and Lily lived, Karen and Carlos got a place with their daughter, Isis. They bonded with Frankie and Mimi; it felt right living close to their trusted new friends. Carlos was dealing coke also. He and Frankie did a fair amount of business together. It was much more profitable than working in a woodshop, as Frankie knew. He was one who was doing quite a bit of coke and getting kind of whacky as a result. Unfortunately, so was Karen, so with a baby on board, Mimi, being grounded in domestic affairs, was often to the rescue to babysit and help out. It became more and more evident why they wanted to live by the stable, hip Frankie and Mimi.

They managed to complete the school year with good grades, amazingly. With everything that was going on, Frankie and Mimi didn't let the fast living keep them from taking care of business, for now.

Like a conductor, Panhandle Pete was looking down on everything from his perch on Guerreo Street. He kept an eye on everything going on but didn't participate in the drug taking. He previously had a bit of a heroin habit in New York, but he had gotten over it and only did acid now. It couldn't have been much fun due to the disability he now lived with due to getting hit in the head. He hired Melvin Belli to sue the hospital that had so wrongly misdiagnosed his major head trauma by telling him he had a "cut in the ear." Unfortunately for Pete, the suit happened at the exact same time the medical malpractice laws came under scrutiny and were changed so that doctors didn't have to carry crazy liability insurance and send the cost of care even higher, so he lost his case.

John was taking off to India for the summer. It was a favorite of his for some reason nobody understood, but he loved the culture. He wasn't there to study religion or hang out with a swami or guru. He would travel around and live cheaply on his modest budget. Frankie would wait for his return to beat him at chess.

The family bought a nice house in Sacramento, big, and they needed a dining table built. Frankie still had a foot in the door at the Coop, through Robert and Malie, and Richard didn't exactly have a grip on reality, so he was able to whip out a nice white Formica-with-leaves dining table. He was up all night doing the work. He loaded it into his '57 Ford truck the next day and took off for Sac. He was coming over the Bay Bridge (on the lower deck, going east, in the shade). By the time he got to Emeryville, the morning sun shone on the white Formica. The contact adhesive in those days was so flammable it burst into flames. Luckily a CHP saw what was going on when he pulled over and had a fire extinguisher at the ready and put out the fire. It was not beyond repair, but it was a rather exciting event. He told them when he got it to them he would bring the necessary stuff to repair the damage next visit. When Frankie worked for Paul, he remembered hearing him tell stories when Richard (from the Coop) had to jump out of windows because of fire due to the extremely flammable glue.

Dana was going to join the Navy. Before he was able to actually join, Frankie still cared enough about his little brother that he took him to meet Took. Took was a very good flamenco guitarist, friend of Antonio. He was a fat black guy, great trained cook, student of many things, who paid the rent and gave him a stipend. He was in the Navy, probably on the GI Bill. He was a great guy with great stories and loved to cook. He was a palm reader. Frankie assumed that he held the current group think way of the world then that said it was bad to join the Navy. It was war and wrong; he was told and had to believe.

"Naw, joining the Navy was probably the best thing I ever did," he said after a couple of lines at his Ninth and Irving hovel.

"Took! I can't believe what I'm hearing. Joining the Navy is like going to jail. Fuck the military. Fuck taking orders from some sadistic asshole sergeant or whatever they call them in the Navy," said Frankie.

"It got me out of a bad situation. I saw the world, learned to cook, and now they're paying my way through school. I loved it," he said.

Frankie just chopped out another fat line and said, "Great," and did a fat one, trying to think about what to say. Nothing to say.

"But threw it overhand, like this, or behind the back, like this," said BBQ. "And we won." He did like going to Day Street Gym playing ball, real street ball, with BBQ. It kind of eased the pain when Frankie realized BBQ just needed food and someone with the means to take care of him. He'd show up and go straight to the fridge, see what there was to eat. Mimi would often cook for him. He needed them. He did have good stories. Until he managed to get his own SSI checks, he raided his mom's and ate at Frankie's.

Betty was done with men, unless they had money. Husband number three, or was it four? She was done with them; she didn't need men. The last one was an exorcism in matrimony. She was a determined single woman with a business of her own. She was in the credit management business. Everybody in Sacramento had to have the biggest, fanciest cars, houses, clothes without the income to pay for it. They had to have a BMW but couldn't afford a Honda on their $20,000-a-year state job. She schooled them all on what had to happen, and it wasn't pretty. She had her own credit counseling business and worked out payment plans so they could keep the fancy stuff.

When Frankie was 8 years old, Arnie and Betty would take him to the Friday Night Races and Hard-Top races in Roseville. It was great fun. They went enough that they got to know one of the drivers, Joe Guieste. He was quite the artist when he was young and sat down and drew a picture of Joe beating his archrival Jim Baker by half a car length, which did happen. Little Frankie gave the picture to Joe, and the next week when he won, he pulled his car up in front of the stands, got out, walked up to the beautiful black-haired trophy girl, gave her a big long kiss (he was kind of greasy and unshaven), lit a cigarette, took the microphone, and said, "Where's my little buddy Frankie? Come down here, Frankie, I got something for you."

"Go on down," said Arnie and pointed to the gate to the track. He made his way down across the sticky dirt track to where they were standing, and Joe gave him the trophy. The trophy girl gave him a peck on the cheek. He was right in the middle of it. Joe was talking dirty to the girl; she was smiling. Frankie was wide-eyed when the picture was taken. He had a trophy.

Being a model and somehow having instilled the importance of photographs at stages of life, Betty wanted her two boys to get together with her at Land Park and take some pictures. She was very stylish at the time, as were the boys. Mimi actually took the pictures, but they did the posing, like a rock band. They were cool. They may have looked hip, but Betty was not hip.

On a Friday night race, a little girl was called upon to be the trophy girl, and Betty went, "Booooooo, booo." Arnie said, "Betty, Betty," trying to get her to sit down and shut up since everybody was frowning at her and the poor little girl had never heard anything like that before. She was already nervous, and to have some crazy lady boo her was not good. Betty had issues. Maybe it reminded her of herself or something. It was deeply buried, and Frankie never knew why.

Mimi moved her potter's wheel to Robert's studio, and they spent more time there. Frankie made a cool belt buckle which he gave to Robert, who was all about hands. He had big old hands. The buckle was silver and brass with two hands opposed lifelines stamped in. It was a present to him. He loved it.

There was an unused piece of land behind Robert's studio with just weeds, so that lent itself perfectly to becoming a garden, which both Frankie and Mimi wanted, and Robert wasn't doing anything with it. He was busy now starting to do his sculpture more in the studio.

Robert, Gordon, and Frankie somehow decided—well, it was Frankie's idea—to go to Jenner by the sea, up the coast, and take some acid. They met at Gordon's house across from the San Raphael Civic Center. Gordon had moved up. He was a well-paid mechanic at a Foreign Auto Repair shop over there and worked on all the rich hippies' cars. Found and bindle under the seat of Jerry Garcia's Volvo sports car, empty, nothing in it. He still had the frizzy-haired unattractive bossy bitch of an old lady who didn't like his friends. They got out of there in his '51 Desoto, in perfect condition, of course, and headed up the coast.

They had a nice Denny's breakfast in San Raphael and were on their way. They dropped the acid; it was strong acid for experienced travelers.

They got to the spot north of Jenner where Highway 1 went up into the hills and the sheep ranch up that way, where the creek came into the sea.

It was pretty much deer trails going upward that the sheep used as well that they walked up and up over. There was finally a trail that took them down to the water, which were big tide pools protected by huge rocks and otherwise big waves crashing on the rocks. The rugged Northern California Coast, untamed, wild. Unbelievable natural beauty.

They found the beach and walked north, becoming one with the ocean, and Gold Coast seals were frolicking in the frothy surf as they watched the intruders on their beach. They walked a mile up the sandy beach, examining the timbers and garbage insoluble to the salty surf, sculpted by Mother Nature herself.

"New horizons," said Robert and gestured to the next point a broken-up mass of huge boulders. There was a high path and a low path. Gordon and Frankie took the high path, and Robert took the low path. They looked out in the afternoon sun at the kelp beds living in the tide, swirling in and out. The seals, sunning themselves on the rocks, began barking. "Look, whales," said Robert. A pod of sperms surfaced and blew their holes for another breath. "Yeah," they said. "We see them."

They climbed the mass of boulders at the point. Gordon got to the top first and straddled it, looking down the other side. He gave Frankie a look of fear and wonder of what to do next. Frankie noticed the look, and when he reached the top, he burst into laughter. Robert, still climbing, looked up at them and said, "What, what is it?" The other half of the huge rock had not broken into smaller boulders. It was still intact, with a sparse bit of vegetation clinging to the face and a 150-foot drop to the beach below. Robert got to the top and smiled at them, looking down at what none of them could have imagined they would see until they saw it. That was as far as they would go that day, no more new horizons. On the way back, the tide had come up and was making one of the points impassable, except between the waves crashing on mossy rocks where the creek was dripping down. They could have easily been carried out to sea had they gotten hit by a wave, but they didn't.

The unsteady scamper across the slippery rocks between waves added an element of danger.

In a protected cove was an inviting large tide pool, and the weather was hot. Frankie took his clothes off and dove in. "Come on in, fuckers, it feels great," said Frankie, in about eight feet of water. They took off their clothes and waded in, Robert careful not to get his hair wet.

Lying on the warm beach in the sun to dry, Gordon came out with the most unexpected revelation. "For a long time, I've been wondering about whether I might be gay. One time Judy and I were in the mountains at an alpine stream. Lying on the rocks, in the sun, beautiful brown body—I couldn't get turned on," he said. Judy was a lesbian living with Judy Reed. She did indeed have a smoking body. The frizzed-out bossy little Jewish broad he now lived with was enough of a turnoff to give anybody a limp dick. "You mind if I suck your dick?" he asked Frankie.

"Go ahead." Just getting out of the cold water and just not being aroused by Gordon sucking on his very small penis, he gave up. "Well, I guess that means you're not gay, huh?" said Frankie.

"Guess not," said Gordon. Robert was fully dressed as he lit a Kool and tried to look the other way. Frankie had to hand it to him; that took balls. Frankie realized that seeming to be liberated or at least be willing to be gay had its consequences, like having guys who were not sure want to experiment with you. Robert would never utter a word about it, ever. He wanted it erased from his memory.

Carlos was making some serious dough, bought a nice new BMW. He was also doing too much coke. He'd disappear for long periods and come back and was sure someone was fucking Karen. Funny, because he was at Vicki's fucking her. It was rumored that she had done a run at the Bunny Ranch, but he didn't know. He was at home one night, and Isis went tumbling down the stairs. He jumped over her to catch her fall and broke his ankle. He was in the hospital for a day, and when he got out, he went right back to four-day binges.

At Vicki's, he crashed hard and fell asleep on his wallet and totally fucked up his back and leg. This time he ended up in the hospital for a while. He was fucked up.

Carlos had only the best painkiller, smack. Having been a junkie and thinking he knew what he was doing, he didn't and OD'd. "Carlos is dead," Karen told Mimi on the phone. They, of course, came to Karen's aid and took care of Isis and whatever else was needed.

Karen had no resources of her own, but her French family came to the rescue in her recovery in the immediate aftermath. Her parents took custody of Isis. Karen fell into a life of working at X-rated bookstores and movie houses and fucking away her pain. She degenerated into a real slut with no longer a reason to live and eventually died in a drug-induced free fall that nobody could do anything about. It was a sad nonintervention.

Carlos and Karen did have a wealthy clientele. Frankie got to know many of them.

Everybody hip was drug involved. You could stop and go to work and continue on; many didn't.

The school year was coming up. Frankie took genetics, jewelry making, gymnastics, and reading. John was back from India, preparing for his term at Cal. He would drive his '59 bug to Berkeley almost daily.

The highlight of the year was Patty Hearst getting kidnapped. There was applause and fists in the air and hope for the revolution to overthrow the wicked government. They were gathered around the TV getting the daily news. The armed struggle was here—kill the bastards. Frankie was just going along with the whole thing, but John, he had true hatred for the establishment, the Hearsts. They were rich and deserved to be punished. Right on. They were very aware of what and where it happened.

Antonio and Frankie went out together to the clubs downtown or in Sausalito that Antonio devoted all his time to finding where all the hot chicks were. They were recruiting for the parties they were having and, if not, to just get a piece of ass. They were quite successful at this, Especially when there was coke involved. They'd follow you anywhere as long as you were stuffing coke up their noses. The disco scene was popular. It was the perfect setting for meeting the coke whores.

His genetics class really got him to thinking, by what he had read, how important it was. Actually, it was eugenics, the application of genetics. Hitler was the foremost eugenicist of their time. He tried to create the Aryan race, the superior race. And he went on without considering what human beings were doing to the quality of human beings that were being allowed to procreate. Anybody could have kids, didn't matter. Whether one was able or should have kids was never considered—the suicide of the species. More and more people were going on to have kids. Even if they were diabetic or had a genetic disease, they were allowed/encouraged to pass these along to the offspring, no problem. We're creating a generation of idiots.

The year 1975 would be another year of adjustment to what had come before. No time after '67, '68, '69, and maybe '70 would have such an impact, and the social change those years in history would, so you couldn't compare them. It would've been nice to have an enormous upheaval of creativity and shock to the culture every year but impossible.

People were getting restless and hungry for more. The swell was rising; it was on the way.

The counter culture was licking its chops, the rest of America watching closely when Haldeman, Ehrlichman, and Mitchell were convicted and got prison terms. John Dean served a couple of weeks but made a career from being a rat. The Vietnam era was over; David Bowie released "Fame." Patty Hearst was captured in a Noe Valley hideout a couple of blocks from Frankie, well after they caught up with Cinque in LA, where they incinerated him and his army. The group watching TV was feeling defeated. It was over. But good TV.

It no doubt was a shot in the arm of the faculty at Cal. They knew they were on their way.

There were bands like Queen, Kraftwerk, Bad Company, Bob Marley, the Tubes (from the city) Bruce Springsteen, Born to Run. It was okay.

It was delivered by KSAN, the hip FM station in town that had morphed out of KMPX. Dave McQueen read the news with a delivery of cynicism and disgust, the immorality of it all. Scoop Nisker, also known as the Purple Poisoner, Joe Carcinogeny, was laughing like a Buddha at their dance into the fire. "If you don't like the news, go out and make some of your own."

It was good that Frankie was in good shape (sleeping normal hours, eating well, not going on binges at the time), and Bobby, from across the street, was knocking on the door at like eight in the morning. "Frankie. Got you a job at the Exploratorium. We're leaving right now. Let's go." He threw on some clothes and ran out to the nice Mercedes 230 the boys were sitting in waiting for Frankie to get in so they could ride down Steiner Street across town to the Marina, where they would take the left to the Palace of Fine Arts building where the museum was located. It was Palace of Fine Arts, a beautiful Greek Doric, mostly. When Bernard Maybeck designed it, he did not hold to the strict guidelines of the architectural definition of Greek Doric, as he did with all the buildings in the bay area and beyond that he designed. He took liberties with the design and mixed and matched a lot. As did Julia Morgan, who came along a little later, who designed Hearst Castle, which strayed far from any rules of design.

"This is Pete. He's the boss. He gets the front seat," said Bobby, as laughter broke out. "Donny and Jamie. They provide the laughter and do the work."

"How do you do?" said Frankie as he shook hands with them. Everybody lived in Noe Valley and was picked up by Bobby in the nice Mercedes (which he bought in New Orleans with funds he won at a horse race that he got a tip on to bet) for the leisurely ride up Steiner to the museum. It was a laugh fest.

The work was building the new administrative offices for museum office staff. Office staff was the usual clerical requirements for running a museum but had the need for fundraisers. Raising funds was what gave the Exploratorium life—a lot of funds.

Pete, the boss, was friends with Frank's son in Colorado when he was a cattle rancher. Frank Oppenheimer was a physicist who worked on the Manhattan Project, as did his probably more famous brother, Robert, on the atomic bomb. He taught and had notable accomplishments in nuclear physics, but what was most notable was that both he and his brother had their doubts about what they had done, and what they had discovered was going to be used to exterminate thousands of people in Hiroshima and Nagasaki with the atomic bomb. Being it was during the McCarthy era, when people were getting accused of being un-American, or even worse, communists, and blacklisted, just like Bill and Silvia, John's parents got caught up.

Jackie, Frank's wife, did, in fact, attend socialist meetings. They bought a ranch in Colorado and raised cattle until 1966 when Frank got the idea to open a museum, a science museum for kids mainly to pull and push and hit and squeeze and even kick to make something happen and learn something. He liked the mischievous nature of kids, a natural teacher. He wanted to see yelling and screaming and kids being kids, skipping from one exhibit to the next to play with it. Touching was encouraged. Brilliant, really.

Frankie was now a construction guy helping to build the offices. Donny and Jamie were a team, clowns really, who made everything funny and knew the most important thing one could was have fun. Building the offices was just a job, though. What they really did was art. They were the Ant Farm. Visual, media, art—they blazed that trail.

It was the bicentennial, so they took a garbage can that was in the Civic Center, painted stars and stripes on it, tied a 2×4-inch to the rope of the tallest flagpole in front of City Hall, put the can on it upside down, ran it up to the top, dropped the can over the top of the pole, brought the 2×4 back down, and untied it in the middle of the night. There was absolutely no one there then; it was before they ruined the beautiful city.

The next day when the sergeant-in-arms came out in the morning to raise the flag to find he couldn't. They had to get San Francisco Fire Department's tallest ladder truck to get it down, of course, turning it into a media event.

They bolted chairs to a building two stories up at Mission and Van Ness, white chairs, and put on all white clothes, painted themselves white, had microphones and speakers, and talked gibberish for many hours. The media came and recorded everything. They didn't even crack a smile. Bobby, Pete, and Frankie sure did when they went to check it out on the way to the museum that morning. They set up a wall of TVs in the Cow Palace parking lot, set it on fire, and ran a '59 Caddy into it. They called everyone they had addicted to their art to take a picture at moment of impact. For a while, there were two freeway overpasses (now Route 92) over 101 with nothing attached to them. No freeways, just the overpasses, over the 101

South. Somehow they dropped a '60 Chevy on the top overpass. It took a sky crane (helicopter) to pick it up from above to get it down. They are the same guys who did the dozen or so Cadillacs with the front halves buried diagonally in a field in Texas. These were some fun guys to work with. Then there was Frank. Frank was a musician at night, so he worked late, playing shit-kicking kind of country, kind of bluegrass, in a working band. During the day, at noon, he was the duckiologist. He protected the ducks in the pond from being terrorized by dogs. And he was, of course, a comedian. The name of his band was Slippery in the Saddle.

Frankie, being an actual carpenter and cabinetmaker, was able to communicate that to Pete when the structure was built. He built the reception desk and other assorted fixtures and shelving in the shop they had right there used to build exhibits and everything else.

He just adjusted his cocaine intake to be during the day when the job had to get done. Getting high was secondary; the work was more fun than you could have getting stupid.

Once that was done, Frankie stayed on to build the museum store, across from the offices. Donny and Jamie had bigger and better things to do. Bobby hooked up with a beautiful woman from New Orleans and dropped Anabelle like a hot rock. She was the creative force behind Plain Dealing. Oh well. Bobby was moving back to New Orleans; he rented out the upstairs to Jamie and the downstairs to Frank and his pretty wife, who sold imported French mountaineering gear and boots, the best in the world. Last you the rest of your life. Frankie bought a pair.

Frankie got Robert a job at the Exploratorium, but Pete didn't like him because he was always taking cigarette breaks and laughing it up with the duckiologist, not getting a lot of work done. It was getting stuff done and then having a good time, not the other way around. Robert wasn't invited to stay and work in the store.

Pete was going to Colorado and left Frankie in charge of building the store. This put him in direct contact with Frank Oppenheimer and Jackie, his wife. Frank was a mad scientist type who drank and chain-smoked, pacing around the place kind of hunched over, thinking, smoking. He would come into the store under construction, look around, bob his head, blink a bit, and leave a trail of smoke swirling in his wake.

The fundraisers were getting results because Frank had good ideas. Among them were new classrooms in a new central structure—built with brick, masonry, permanent-like. In the circular structure that housed the classrooms, there were 3×6-foot windows in the classrooms. Well, of course, they needed to make them so you couldn't just look into the classrooms. With all that money, you had to have stained glass windows to obscure the view. They had Artists in Resident money and commissioned a stained-glass artist. He wasn't there much, but his cute frizzy-haired beauty from who knows where came in to do the actual work. Having to walk past her back and forth while she was doing her work (cutting pieces of colored glass for the windows), it could not be helped that he and she would have dialogue. He was over at her place in a day or two. After dinner at her really cool living situation in Seacliff in a big house with a lady and her daughter, they made it to her bedroom on the top floor with a view of the bridge. She said, "Suck my breasts." That was not a problem. Frankie did as she asked and then gave it to her good. They were young and came. It was beautiful.

Then there was Jeanette. Jeanette was a graphic artist and a recent hire by Graphics. She was long and tall and good-looking and lived in Mill Valley. It was the dawning of the age of sexual freedom. There was a whole thing going on with peacock feathers and hot tubs; her husband was involved somehow. Frankie was none too impressed with any of it. Jeanette was definitely fuckable, however. It wasn't long before Frankie, from the jobsite, didn't exactly say he liked her ass but something like that, to which she answered, "That will get you everywhere," as she walked by. After a while, she left her husband, probably because he was fucking someone else. She moved into a rustic house at the very top of Mount Tam with the ultimate view. He went up there from time to time to give it to her good.

The building that the Exploratorium was in surrounded the famous rotunda. It was built in 1914 to celebrate the Panama Canal completion, the rebuilding of San Francisco from the destruction from the fire that resulted from the 1906 earthquake and the World's

Fair. It was a big deal—a massive construction project with dozens, if not hundreds of buildings running from the Civic Center all the way up Van Ness then to the Palace of Fine Arts from Fort Mason, all the way from what is now the Marina, all built with the earthquake itself freshly in their minds but still to be torn down after the World's Fair. The Palace of Fine Arts building surrounding the rotunda (from the top view, plan view, a half circle), a half circle built with a hinge at the ridge with two trusses on both sides, making half of the roof and either the inside or outside walls. Impossible to fall down in the event of an earthquake or just about anything else, it was steel trusses and plaster inside and out, inflammable. That did not get torn down, along with, of course, the rotunda. The plaster they used on the dome and the giant angels did not last and had to be redone in 1966. The molds to cast the entire structures were stored inside the outer utilitarian building, behind all the tanks and military hardware they needed to store during WWII, the Presidio and Fort Mason being right there. And it had a full-size theater at the south end of the building.

Jackie (Frank's wife) and Anabelle, her best friend, were a couple of older ladies who sat at a desk in the Graphics Department with a big glass window right in front of the entrance/walkway into the museum. They didn't miss a thing; they saw everything. In fact, what they said went that way. They were in charge. But that was okay if they liked you.

They had control of the original pictures taken of the fabulous structure in the day, phenomenal. The lighting was all working. If you ever see any of these pictures, you'll know these people, Frankie's ancestors, were building Rome in 1907 to 1914.

For some reason, Panhandle Pete moved out of his beautiful pad overlooking the world and moved into a middle-class nice-enough house on Ulloa, off Sloat. He moved in with a sweaty little fellow named Mario. He was a city-employed gardener in Golden Gate Park who was a drop-dead deadhead and loved coke. Had to have it. He began frequenting Frankie's place for gram after gram after gram. Frankie began to realize this was not just the case with Mario.

Several people, who had no self-control of their own, used Frankie to regulate their consumption by coming by three times a day. To them, Frankie said, "I'm not selling anything less than an eighth of an ounce."

Antonio was in Spain studying flamenco dance. In between his jaunts to Amsterdam and Paris, he was no doubt getting high-quality European poontang. He never paid for it or for drinks or for coke even; he had parties. He was in control and pretty much always kept his nose out of it. When he was here, he would throw a party, almost always at J Tony Serra's house or the fancy offices and homes at his rich lawyer friends. Frankie was always available to get some hot chicks to attend, provide security (Malie), and bring the coke. They had an especially good party at a big beautiful house in San Raphael with a big pool and everything. The parties always featured a bowl of punch laced with acid, very strong, and a tank of nitric oxide. The nitric oxide was usually in a bedroom or something and would always attract a crowd. Antonio would walk in the room after making the rounds and acknowledging everyone and pleased his guests with his regal presence. Everyone would stand back from the tank. He would walk over to the tank and put the tube in his mouth. The music would change to a flamenco or with a Latin signature, and he would take an endless hit. People ooohhhed and aaahhhed, and he would walk out for another tour.

So as he finished the construction of the store, Frankie started seeing the advantages of working at the Exploratorium and was able to prove to the powers that be that they needed him.

Jackie Oppenheimer, wife of Frank, was that power and ran Graphics. Graphics was where everything was drawn so it could be built, like the exhibits and signage stands, to explain the exhibit, and nice custom shelving, desks, whatever Jackie and Anabelle needed. They smoked Parliaments and ran the place from there.

Frankie fit right in. They gave him a desk right across from them so he could get a bit of the view they had too, and of course, he was going to need a bench in the shop.

The shop was already pretty crowded with people who helped think up the exhibits and build them; they were very talented, hip, or at least ponytailed and were a very territorial bunch. They spent a lot of time drinking coffee, looking through catalogs, and generally didn't want to be interrupted from making sure to keep themselves in work by not doing anything and didn't like "new guys." Richard, a nerdy machinist and member of the club, said, "No, I'm not moving my bench. There's no room." Tom, another exhibit builder and catalog reader, said, "There's no room for another bench here," and walked into his nook in the open office cluttered with exhibit parts and crap where he did the coffee drinking with the club.

"They tell me there's no room in the shop for the bench," said Frankie to Jackie in her perch in Graphics.

She said, "Oh yeah, we'll see about that," and marched over to the shop with Frankie behind. She walked up to Richard, Tom, and Joe (the guy with the title foreman), pointing to an area between Richard's bench and a work table, and said, "You," looking at Richard. "Move that bench that way, and Frankie's bench is going right there. Got it!" Nobody said a thing. The little Irish woman walked away, the bench got moved, and Frankie got a nice new bench. He shot the government General Services table, supplied in abundance, into the asphalt floor with power actuated stud gun.

Frankie and Mimi were flying over the Bay Bridge on their way to Marguirette's to take a sauna and hot tub at about eighty-five miles per hour on the lower deck to Berkeley, and she said, "Got the car up to a hundred ten on the bridge the other day."

"You got the car up to a hundred ten miles per hour?" said Frankie as he looked at her quizzically. She put her fist in her mouth and looked out the window. That would be if there was something wrong with some outside cock for her to enjoy when Frankie wasn't around. She couldn't say his name, but it was clear some young stud got his hands on her car and was driving at a high rate of speed, 110 miles per hour. He smiled and didn't say anything. He would leave the openness of their relationship unspoken because he sure as hell was taking full advantage of its openness. He figured it would be best to let sleeping dogs lie.

It's not like he was insecure about it, but he wanted to be number one. He knew he was. He should pay attention to what he had, not to mention she was worth about twenty million when her grandpa expired. He owned National Gypsum, then worth about a billion. That really didn't matter to him; he was, in fact, liberated in some ways and would never have or not have a relationship with anyone for those reasons. He was above that and very idealistic.

With the museum store done, the fun stuff for sale had been sold at the original store, and the new fun stuff was selected by Jackie and Anabelle and, of course, ordered, organized, displayed, and all that by Nancy. Nancy was a surrogate daughter of sorts to Jackie, who ran the store. She was another avid deadhead who smoked pot in the back room. Frankie got Mimi a job there; it was perfect for her. She was good at the displays and with the kids, doing the sales, and the related activity going on in a museum with that kind of store.

Chet moved from the place on Twenty-Fourth with Foot out to the early Avenues. It was a dumpy place on a flat lot with overgrown shrubbery and a yard for Foot and his roommate's dog, Trax. Trax was one of those psycho huskies totally out of control, the control of John Dean. This John was a painter and an illustrator and a coke fiend. Frankie and John Dean became friends over it, and he lived with Chet, who didn't approve. In fact, he was kind of a pain in the ass about it. People he knew had gone down doing it, blah, blah, blah. He was actually right to say it was not what they wanted. No one listened. It was right here, and it got you high. Great.

John Dean was a very intense guy. One time Frankie surprised him when he came by to show Chet some pot, and not just tweaking, he was mad, like crazy. "Hey, John, what's happening?" said Frankie. The door was open, and he was standing by his drawing board, looking like Mr. Hyde, with a gruesome smile. He was just fucked up, but he was deeply rooted in drug making and getting really high. He did have the best acid known to man, or at least the strongest, way stronger than Panhandle Pete's. The shit Frankie would get from John Dean was for the experienced connoisseur only, definitely five hundred mics a hit. While Frankie was peddling low yield pot to Chet, who struggled to pay anyone who fronted him anything, John Dean was figuring out how to press acid into double barrels and make "Broken Sunglass" acid, which was on kelp squares and looked like small pieces of tinted sunglass lenses. Like everyone else, he was always needing coke and became another one Frankie had to say "I don't sell anything less than an eighth" to. He had an unlimited supply of one-hundred-dollar bills.

Mark and Cybil were making the rest of the family very uncomfortable with their antics, and Marguirette had never had to be confrontational or tell her daughter and her scumbag boyfriend to get out, but Frankie didn't have a problem with it. "You and Mark are going to have to find someplace to go because you can't stay here," he told Cybil. Mimi or Marguirette could have never done that, but that was what they wanted.

Mark came upstairs and said angrily, "Did you just tell Cybil to get out of here, Frankie?"

"Yeah, they want you out of here," said Frankie. Before he knew it, Mark coldcocked him, right in the eye, very hard, and ran downstairs. Frankie went into the bathroom to examine his eye, which was already blackening and bad. Frankie went downstairs, kicked the door to the bedroom open, went in, grabbed Mark, threw him on the floor, got his head between his legs, and beat the living shit out of him. It was funny. Mark was trying to say, "Frankie, what are you doing?" To which Frankie said, "I'm going to kill you," Frankie always did want to get a good look at Cybil's nice big young natural tits and did when she came out of the shower and pulled Frankie off Mark. It was good that she did because Frankie would have killed him. He just made a bloody mess out of his face. They left.

Frankie zipped out to Brisbane to have a puff with Robert and Tough John for a Schlitz and a Vodka Grape for John. They raced their sports cars on the edge of death and disaster on the well-banked and built-for-high-speed section of connector over the San Bruno mountains—Guadalupe Canyon Road. Scenes from the movie *Bullitt* were filmed there. So it had been there for a while. Tough John was going to put a Chevy 350 in an Austin Healy "bug-eyed" Sprite. He was going to mop the floor with these guys. Gordon was child rearing in San Raphael, unaware of the race he could have won.

Frankie was home one Saturday, and the doorbell rang. It was Michael. "Michael, what ya doin? What you got there?"

He held up a beautiful bud of weed and said, "Grew some pot. Wanna smoke some?"

"You grew this? Where?" he asked.

"Hawaii, I just got off the plane a couple of hours ago," he said.

"Hawaii? You live in Hawaii now?"

"Yup," he said. He had moved to Hawaii with a hundred hits of acid to make a buck to survive for a while. He gave the hits to a guy he met, in Kona, to sell. They walked out to the beach, where a big Hawaiian was, and he took the acid and punched the guy out.

He got a job in a restaurant and bought a four-wheel-drive truck. He drove the truck around the big island and planted marijuana plants in many locations, which he tended, even with the loss of 80 percent of the crop to deer and maybe thieves. Not many people knew that pot was a plant and could be grown like a plant. Of course they knew nothing about history, hemp, or anything, still don't, let alone what a marijuana plant looked like. He still got 20 percent, which amounted to several pounds at least.

"Eleven hundred dollars a pound!" said Michael.

"Eleven hundred dollars a pound? You gotta be kidding," said Frankie. "For that it must be good. Let's smoke a joint," he said as the doorbell rang.

It was Pogo, the country boy from schoolhouse territory. He always wanted to be in the middle of it. "Pogo, what's going on?" asked Frankie.

He was always smiling. A logger and lumberjack, red-faced from working outside, he held out a big beautiful bud of weed and said, "Growing pot, want to smoke some?" He walked into the living room, and Frankie introduced the two. "Where's your tray?" he said.

"I got it right here. I happen to be rolling one at the moment," said Michael.

"Let's smoke some of this," said Pogo.

"This is something Michael grew in Hawaii," said Frankie. "We'll smoke some of yours in a minute. How much is your pot, Pogo?" asked Frankie.

"A thousand dollars a pound," he said.

Even though both were "sinsemilla" (no balls, no seeds—more production of THC not having seeds to produce was the theory), Frankie was not that impressed. It was okay. His people were used to paying $350 a pound. He'd take some and try to sell it but wasn't really encouraged by it.

In Brisbane, he was hanging out with Robert and Tough John, playing some boccie and having a couple Schlitzes while Robert worked in the studio on his California Girl sculpture. California Girl was Robert doing a version of Judy Reed he remembered fondly. She had a face that changed as it went through the process of him working on it. She was tall and lean, very lean, if not skinny, with hands on her hips, long legs with bell-bottom pants, big bell-bottoms. Then he got to rocking it back and forth on her feet. He went too far a couple of times, and it landed on the arms sticking out the back. He broke the arms numerous times then figured out to inset lead in the feet so it didn't fall over, but he tried. In between the boccie and working in the studio, there was time to joke around and make fools of themselves. Robert leaned over to the crotch of a good-sized plum tree in the yard by the bocci ball court, which did look like a vagina. He sniffed and smiled, looking at the two knowingly. They burst into laughter.

Tough John was about to marry a cutesy little bubblehead from Daly City and was getting good poontang when he hadn't passed out from too many Vodka Grapes. They got on the subject of "pussy farts," which he heard for the first time. Frankie went a bit further and blew air in there and listened to the music. Quaffing was something they would always talk about from that time on. They were actually looking for a way to can them and would greet each other as if opening a can with air in it and make the sound it would make—*buuuusssshhhh*. It was always a greeting of joy. Dirty bastards.

Joni left Arnie, which didn't mean much to Frankie other than to free him up for the hot broad across the street to let her car roll out of the driveway and into his fence. She probably did it on purpose. He was pretty desirable. Nice house, gray hair, getting longish, drove a Mercedes convertible, single. Frankie knew he hadn't forgotten or forgiven him for having left and been gone all that time, with no word. Frankie understood. Arnie would let it seep out and still be a dick. Dana was in Japan in the Navy.

BBQ would come by and get Frankie for some Gorilla Ball at Day Street Gym. They were actually pretty good and won some games. They'd go across the street to Hondo's place afterward and hang out, maybe watch a game. Hondo was the youngest of three brothers with no front teeth. The whole family was tough, not Malie tough but tough. The oldest was Ed. He was the toughest.

Hondo was a rigger in the shipyard and known to drink with his buddies and stumble home. He knew Frankie's place, having come to a couple card games, and one night, he came stumbling by and knocked on the door. The little hulk was indeed incapacitated and would not have made it four blocks. Frankie got him inside, gave him coffee and a line, wiped his face with a cool wet cloth, and sent him on his way home to his wife and kid.

Ed made a point to thank Frankie for looking after brother Hondo. Ed did a stretch at San Quentin for having dished out an ass whooping that put him away for some years, but out now, he had a nice little clock repair/restoration shop a few blocks away. Given it was San Francisco and with its history, a clock shop was much more than a clock shop. Beautiful 150-year-old clocks, nice stuff—he knew how to make them work, a handy prison education gone right.

Many a night was spent with John (back from India, going to Berkeley), Robert, Michael, and whoever else had a day off here and there to go on chess-playing marathons in Frankie's living room. They listened to Peter Frampton's "Sail Away," Fleetwood Mac, and discovered Iggy Pop's *New Values*. The sun would come beaming in the beautiful dark green room with high ceilings, the same Indian silk tapestry that hung from the Hermann Street ceiling, eclectic art on the walls, Belgian carpets, antiques. The acid-taking slowed and the coke-snorting increased, the morning sun was not welcome. The light shined on their conversation that didn't amount to more than babbling. Mimi wasn't always around. She would go on trips to Disneyland and Bora, Bora with the family. She missed some of the stupidity, but not all of it, she came back from those trips to partici-pate enough. Bet she wished she hadn't.

At the museum, Frankie was not liked too much by the group who didn't like change in the shop. Not only did he invade their space, they didn't like the way he dressed (even though he hardly wore anything flashy or shiny; it was work, where one made dust, got dirty) or wore his hair (no ponytail). He didn't like or respect them either; he didn't answer to them. Too bad, he was in. He worked for Graphics.

The first exhibit he built for them was designed by a graphic designer in Graphics, Larry Antila. He was very good, very professional, and Frankie didn't bother him. He liked him. It was called the *Thermograph*. The thermograph was a very early camera that showed hot as light (white) and cold as black on a black and white TV monitor. Having to be kidproof, it was a freestanding aluminum-framed plywood cabinet with molded clear Plexiglas front behind where the TV monitor sat. The back was an aluminum door to access it. It was made to incorporate the look of an English sports car. It looked fast. They put a block of ice in front of it so you could put your hands on and hold up to the thermograph. It looked like you had black paint on your hands.

Not everyone in the shop had a stick up their ass. Kevin, an Amerasian kid from Marin who had a long braided ponytail and wore special high-top moccasins made of buffalo skin, an apprentice to the coffee-drinking, catalog-reading assholes, was cool. Kevin was really their gopher, who was learning things from these fools. He was fascinated by Frankie and helped him. They'd become friends over time, over drugs, coke really. He was a smart kid with a natural mechanical aptitude, which Frankie was familiar with, and he could weld.

Bob Miller was the most important artist at the Exploratorium. He designed and built the *Light Spectrum*, truly ingenious and beautiful. From the roof of the building, he figured out how to track the direct image of the sun across the sky and direct that very bright light beam down to the floor of the museum. Bouncing off another mirror, that light beam was sent through a series of prisms. Thirty-three-foot prisms hung in a four-foot-long panel in a metal rack cordoned off from the floor of the museum. The light would be broken up into all the colors of the spectrum. The most vivid, pure colored light broken into indigo, blue, green, red, yellow. Unbelievable. Every once in a while, some rowdy kid would climb under the barrier and push the swinging panel, redirecting the refracted light spectrum to another series of mirrors, and the most unbelievable light show ever seen would light up the entire dark huge museum building. Wow. Its purpose was to go through a series of a three-foot-high-by-four-foot-wide panel of mirrors to then be directed to big (kid-tolerant) opaque plastic screens and Mylar panels, further breaking up the colors. The kids were bathed in colored light, and it was beautiful. The logo (insignia) of the museum was the rainbow, that rainbow.

Bob was Franke's favorite, and for good reason; the guy was the smartest in the barn. Not only was he the smartest, he was the most creative, innovative. He was right in the middle of the club with a small desk but really didn't participate in the club's hunts. Whoever they didn't like occupied their time without doing any actual work on the museum's business.

Bob liked Frankie, and he was a good cabinetmaker, so he got his help building his next exhibit, the *Walk-In Kaleidoscope*. It was a triangular-shaped structure that had three front surfaced mirrors about four feet tall and six feet wide on the inside. The mirrors were about four feet off the floor so one ducked down under the bottom rail to stand up inside and see your image to infinity. It was very interesting. There was also *Everyone Is You and Me*. It was a small table with two built-in seats facing one another. In the center of the table between the two people sitting looking at one another was a piece of glass transmitting of light, as it was reflective, mirrored. Each side had two lights shining on the subjects and dimmer switches for each hand. You aligned your noses and played with the brightness. It was especially interesting to do with your father or mother. Twins really caught everyone's attention when a pair sat down at it. Trippy, for sure. Momentarily, you forgot what you looked like.

A close second favorite of Frank's was Bill Parker. He was formerly a professor of physics at MIT and was a glassblower and did neon lighting. Frankie wondered why he only worked at night. Bill came up with the *Star Sculpture*. It was a glass ball (orb) a little larger than a basketball in which it was a gaseous medium and electrically charged to emit a luminous glow that conducted to your hands when touched as well as danced around inside, resembling soft colored lightning. He worshipped Nikola Tesla. From Vermont, he was sitting under a tree in a storm when he was a kid, and the tree was struck by lightning. Changed him forever.

The year 1976 would see the United States, the USSR, China, and France, of course, setting off nukes all over the fucking place to show their might. Patty Hearst, or Tania, would get convicted for robbery and sentenced to seven years. OJ Simpson, who played for Buffalos (and San Francisco City College), would rush for 273 yards in one game, and the badass Israeli commandos pulled off the raid on Entebbe.

Stupid bands like Kiss and AC/DC would come into being, but what was important to Frankie was that bands like the Sex Pistols, the Ramones, and Blondie would hit the music scene by storm. Being twenty-two, Frankie was a Punk himself, identified with the new music of rebellion. The wave had crested, and it was coming now.

The party circuit in town was frequented by three hot chicks whom everybody knew and wanted to get—Debbie, Darlene, and Dora, blondes with shags, short skirts, high boots, smoking bodies, and a hard catch. BBQ was rejected by Debbie and somehow made him look like a fool in front of a bunch of people sitting at a table at Bimbo's during a show, which wasn't hard, and he threw a drink in her face. The glass, he said, slipped out of his hand and hit her in the lip, cut her lip. He was arrested and somehow got the charges dropped later after he spent some time in jail. Good thing he was a fast talker; he got out of that one.

Frankie caught her, though. She lived right down the street. He would get away and bang her when he could, and he could, she was hot. No falling in love allowed. She had parties, and everyone was invited, except BBQ.

Panhandle Pete was back in New York, making real money dealing acid.

The kids (Frankie, Mimi, and Adrianna) took a trip to Monterey to see the new generation of race cars. Pursuing auto racing wouldn't be new for Frankie; he was introduced to it by Arnie and Betty, at the Hard Tops, in Roseville. It was gas; what was not to like about it? "Let's go to Laguna Seca. You'll love it," he assured them. It was fun. They discovered the corkscrew part of the track, and made a picnic out of it. That year, David Hobbs, a Brit, was driving the baddest-ass 3.0 CSL BMW designed to beat Porches. He jumped out in the lead, fouled a spark plug, had to come in the pits, get it fixed, came out a lap down in front of the Porches that were now leading, came all the way around in twenty-six laps, and came in second. It was a real thrill; he was hooked.

Pogo was off to South America to get some coke and smuggle it back. Upon his return, he expected Frankie to sell it for him; he didn't know anyone else. Frankie eventually did, since everybody was so crazy for it, but it burned like hell. It had a bad final wash. Once he did sell it, he was off to do it again.

It never occurred to Frankie that some of these people hanging around might be taking advantage of his generosity with coke. He was stuffing large amounts up a lot of noses. Easy come, easy go, he figured. It amounted to thousands of dollars, nevertheless.

Larry Marshall, King Kong's guitarist, was hanging around. If it was free, he was there. So even though he didn't like coke that much, he did like pot, and Frankie's was free. His dad was black, and his mom was Jewish. He looked white, and the rest of the family looked black. Larry was six feet, four inches and white and didn't look at all like his scrawny five-foot-six black dad. Early on they lived in the projects on Army and Folsom Streets, which were all black. Looking white, he got his ass kicked and was the ugly duckling in the family, so his mom protected him as much as she could. He otherwise grew into a big kid and turned out to be pretty tough, but he was the cheapest motherfucker Frankie ever met. Getting over on people was like a sport to him; he lived for not paying and getting someone else to. It was a perfect match because Frankie was giving it all away. Larry was a good friend.

Larry grew up with Paul, a local guy that came around to buy a gram once in a while. He was a biker who lived in a very old rundown house behind a very big old rundown house inhabited by Stan and Steve, twins, who also grew up with Larry and didn't like him much. Stan and his brother were hot rodders and had a shop on the ground floor of the big house where they worked on cars. They also had a huge slot car track, which, of course, provided hours of entertainment for the twins and their friends. Stan and Frankie hit it off and became buddies, and Frankie got invited to the Wednesday night races. Most twins were totally connected, but these two hated each other. Stan was bigger and meaner, and Steve almost got his ass kicked at one of these races. It was serious business. Stan was a good guitarist and had a record collection of every rock record ever put out. Bizarre genres like Big-Time Wrestling, banned underground black humor, Dr. Demento, and now Punk.

The latest exhibit was a table to sit at and experience the Ishihara color test, the color blindness test. Graphics Larry designed a beautiful freestanding hexagonal-sided mushroom-looking table. Being dark in the museum, it was a center birch plywood shaft sixteen inches in diameter with a white Formica and birch tabletop dividers, built with matching birch benches. Light shined up from inside the base through a hole in a clear Plexiglas top in the center onto a cone-shaped mirror and shed the light down onto the tabletop. The Ishihara color test was holding up an either yellow, red, green paddles to look through to see a series of numbers embedded in a series of small circles. Red would cancel out the blue and yellow and let your eye see the red number 7. It all made sense when you did it. But not really. It raised an even more important question, What is the difference between what colors actually exist and what colors your eyes see? There was a lot to know about color and what one saw. The colored paddles slid into slots in a round birch top connected by cables. Otherwise, the little bastards would have stolen them. But they learned something; that was good.

Pete was not only a construction guy, able to build the office and anything else needing to be built, and friend of the son of Frank, he was also an artist, a very creative person.

Frankie was now a color guy and someone with cabinetmaking skills. Pete selected him to help him with an exchange of art pieces or sculptures with the Museum of Modern Art in Civic Center, *Color Collaboration.*

It was a bench facing a white wall about twelve feet away, with a yellow, red, and green (or was it blue?) lights shining on the wall. There was an eight-foot bench, one light at one end, one at the other, and one in the middle. Hanging from the ceiling was a long flexible shaft with a small motor attached to the bench side with a cable. It rotated in the shaft at the other end. A twelve-inch-in-diameter cylinder screen (1/4-inch bars, one inch spaced) floated back and forth. The intersection of the colors and the shadows created all colors, a trip. Genius, really. True color collaboration, every color there is. Interference patterns, light, color. He was seeing colors. It was fun to watch how a guy from Colorado, fishing and being a mechanic out of necessity, used what he knew to make it happen. Flexible fishing leaders that swiveled in order to make the cylinder rotate—nice.

The ponytailed coffee drinkers would have loved to watch Frankie fail but had to watch what was happening. They had to give it to him for having some talent—not as much as they did but some. It was family, with Frank and Jackie at the top, and the hierarchy came on down from the top. Frankie and Mimi, working with Nancy, were accepted as part of the hip family that made up the staff.

Why Frank and Jackie had a large black Labrador or German shepherd attack dog wasn't clear. Its name was Orestes. Orestes was the devil dog, the only dog allowed into the museum. He would attack any other dog. He was mean, big, and black. Frank and Jackie were slight old people that were dragged along by the leash of the powerful animal, so when it was time to take him out to do his business in the green belt along Doyle Drive and the parking lot, Frankie attended to that by taking him out for them. Having taken Kelly to obedience school meant he knew how to train dogs, but this one did whatever the fuck he wanted to.

Punk rock was so new it had no venue yet. Frankie and Mimi were still in disco mode and would go to North Beach to rip up the dance floor. Hot and thirsty, they drank plenty of gin and tonics at the club after a few at Enrico's. Frankie got fucked up. They parked on the other side of the Chinese school on lower Broadway. While walking through the recently paved playground, he was twirling around with his arms outstretched, looking at the sky. The ground eventually smacked him in the face, very hard and very painfully. "Oh, Frankie," was all Mimi could say when she looked at his face in the light of the car with a pained look on her face that said, "This ain't good." He had to peel his bloody face off the pillow in the morning; it was glued to it with dried blood. Once he made it to the bathroom and took a look, he said, "Oh shit."

The loose grit from the fresh asphalt was embedded in the swollen infected abrasion on the side of his face, and there was a cut on the brow where the ground punched him. It was ugly. Not to mention he had a vicious hangover. The custom-made white velvet suit was covered in blood, ruined.

Robert and Adrianna were having a few people over, so they went to Brisbane. "Jesus," said Robert as he turned away, unable to look, but he was laughing.

"Holy shit! What happened to you?" said Tough John as he came in with his girlfriend. There was a doctor who lived nearby and came to the house to take a look. Frankie was looking right into the guy's face reading his pained unconscious half grin like what he was hurt just looking at it, and this guy was a doctor, used to blood and guts. "Yeah, this is bad. You should have gotten stitches here," he said, looking at the cut on the brow. "And this is infected. You better keep it clean," he said.

Being as vain as he was and worried about his beautiful face, he had to keep it clean and drenched in vitamin E for a couple of days, then he had to face work. Everybody stared, but Jackie laughed. She was a rough-and-tumble Irish broad and liked her men rough and tumble too. She thought it was great.

Frankie was at the museum late one night, and in came Bill Parker and a smoking hot companion with red hair, wearing a tight shiny gold suit with heels on. No one else was there, but if there had been, she'd be out of place. But it was Frankie; he'd seen a lot. Not much shocked him. "Hey, Bill, what's happening?" he said as he walked into his area, cluttered with tanks of various gases, glassblowing equipment, and large glass globes. He gave a smile and said, "Frankie, hi." He was there to work, supposedly, with this hot chick, ready to party. "I'm here to work on an exhibit," he said. Yeah, right. "Angie," she said. "Hi, Frankie."

"British, huh?"

"Yes," she said admiringly. Frankie was mostly looking at this thing's great ass when Parker said, "*Electron Beam*."

"What?" said Frankie. "The exhibit, *Electron Beam*." Bill proceeded to explain how the thick glass cylinder, six inches in diameter and four feet long, with big aluminum end caps with a bunch of apparatus with wiring running in and out of it, was a medium in which the forces of nature he had captured in the right amounts made the electrons glow and let you see them illuminate. Frankie could see why this English hottie liked him. He was smart and witty.

"So Bill, want a toot?"

His eyes lit up. He looked at Angie with a knowing smile and said, "Yeah, love one."

"Angie?" Frankie handed her his portable snorting device. "It's loaded. Hold your finger over this hole and take it off and snort." She did and handed it back. Frankie reloaded the "bullet" and handed it to Bill. Frankie would be friends with the two of them separately for a long time as they emptied the bullet and talked in the empty museum.

John Dean, Mr. Hyde, was making some acid of his own and lots of money. He wasn't letting on exactly what he was doing, but once he got to trust Frankie a little more, he was coming by for gram after gram with just a little paranoia. There seemed to be an unlimited supply of the crisp hundred-dollar bills. "John, I'll give you a break on a quarter ounce," said Frankie.

"No, that's okay. I don't want to do too much. I'll get it by the gram. I don't mind paying," he said. There was not much he could do about it; the guy did whatever he wanted. It didn't matter that Frankie was a little uncomfortable with him coming over five times a day.

Stan and Frankie did a fair amount of business together and became good friends. More importantly, Stan respected Frankie, and he didn't have respect for too many people. His house was a monument to the bizarre. He was interested in early freak show stuff, medieval weaponry, and grotesque masks. It was a dump. It looked like the outside, not touched by a paintbrush for at least fifty years.

It was also a year that saw them as a culture that does not necessarily grow up as much as lose their innocence. The decadence followed in a time of celebration and more celebration and more celebration. Bruce Jenner became a new American hero as much as an Olympic champion in '76.

The *Berkeley Barb* reported Timothy Leary had surfaced at a *Star Trek* convention in Oakland to peddle his book *I Grock Spock*. When asked what he thought of Eastern religion, he said, "Nothing good has come out of Asia since the Japanese camera." The *Barb* was all over the new conspiracy, "Reagan's the New Nixon." Of course, he was governor at the time. A lengthy article was written to prove he had direct ties to CREEP (Nixon's Committee to Reelect the President) and on and on. They wanted the truth to be what they wished it was, so you better believe it.

The funniest of all was the full-page insert of the renowned rag for Kool cigarettes with a litho ink of a couple of groovy, happy couples, one frolicking in the water under a waterfall while another pair smoked Kool filters on the edge watching, smiling. That was all right, though it was different for them. They were so much more moral and cared more than you could ever know and devoted the back half to massage parlors with "cute white girls just waiting for you, at low rates, come on down." They did everything but jump off the page and suck your dick. Half holier than thou, half pimp.

Arnie took full advantage of the new liberation and got himself a little girlfriend, younger than Frankie. She was a state worker of some kind. She was cute and squeaky, not very bright, perfect for Arnie. Still didn't smoke weed.

So alternative lifestyles became more mainstream, especially in San Francisco, and people were better adjusted to the liberation of things that kept people hung up. They weren't so hung up anymore; it was good. It meant they were free, free from what bound them to the traditional lives their parents lived, and they even loosened them up a little by now.

Arnie and Jason, the younger half brother who was still only about ten, came to the City to see a Giants game. They stayed the night in Mimi's room, with clean sheets and all that. They were good hosts with no overt drug taking. That would come before and after their visit.

Kevin, the young hipster at the museum, apprentice, gopher to the coffee drinkers, showed up there with a Ducati 350 cafe racer motorcycle. "Nice bike, into bikes heh. Looks fast," said Frankie.

"Oh yeah, anything fast," he said.

"I like fast too. That's my MGA out there," said Frankie.

"I wondered who owned that. Nice," he said. "We'll have to take a drive up Highway 1 sometime."

"Sounds good. I'll be looking forward to it." He had made the most of his education in the metal shop, machine shop, and woodworking technology he had learned. He was smart, industrious young guy. He knew things Frankie didn't, a good guy to know.

Frankie, by now, had explored all of Mimi's anatomy thoroughly through every orifice. He tied her up with silk ropes; had her spread everything to its maximum in various red dresses, miniskirts, knee-high boots, crotchless panties, black trimmed nippleless bras; and took pictures of the fun. Fueled by alcohol and cocaine, "never had to worry about time going byeyeye," they were a little shaky when they made it to work a couple of times, but it was worth it. They settled into a new morality. They weren't hung up like they were before, they thought.

Across from the museum shop was electronics. It was three or four geeks. Before, there were geeks who built electronics-related exhibits.

Frankie noticed a new addition to their staff. He was building an exhibit in the electronics area and building a table for it as well. "Look out, they're doing woodwork in electronics now, are they?"

The new guy laughed nervously, smiled, and said nothing. A couple of days later, the guy was still working on the exhibit. Frankie walked up and said, "Hey, looks good. My name is Frankie. How's it going?" and stuck out his hand.

"Ripley," he said and shook his hand.

"What's this exhibit about?" asked Frankie. "It displays static electricity. If you crank this, it rotates and produces static electricity."

"You came up with this?" asked Frankie. "I suppose you make your own signs and don't need Graphics to make you any," he added, pointing to Graphics, half joking and half fucking with the guy.

"Larry's working on that for me. Thanks."

Pete, the boss, lived right up the hill and stopped in on occasion and, of course, got offered a line or two. He liked it well enough, was married, and had a daughter. He was pretty straight. He invited Frankie to go abalone diving on the north coast. The biology lab did some of their own diving to collect specimens for display and had the necessary diving gear that was available for Frankie to borrow for the dive.

It took a bit of negotiating the swells in the kelp beds, but Pete was able to give him the things he needed to know to get a couple of abalones. Once you spot one that was over six inches in diameter, wait for the surge to carry you away, and when it carried you back, you hung on and plied the unsuspecting mollusk off the rock when you got there and put it in your net.

While diving in Timber Cove, they noticed a guy eager to talk to them, a normal-looking white guy with brown hair. "Hey, hi, how ya doin'? Hey, ya got a net I can borrow?" They were bobbing up and down in the surge and busy doing something else. What could this person want? They got to the rocks and the guy without paying much acknowledgement to the fact they were there diving for abalone, grabbed their gear, and dove in, obviously gathering the abalone they left. He came up with a net full, swam to near where they were, took his many abs out of the net, and took off. Didn't say goodbye, didn't say thanks, just took off. They had enabled a poacher and gave him the equipment to rip off everybody. He was contributing to the shortage, in a big way, by harvesting all the abs he could get then selling them to the local restaurants and the Japanese for sushi at the expense of the rest of them. Pure greed.

Word got out that Ripley was from Vermont. Bill Parker was from Vermont. Nobody left Vermont. Parker went to MIT and had a few degrees. Ripley was self-taught, like most people in Vermont. Ripley's father was an inventor, like many in Vermont, and had made and lost fortunes with his inventions. Rip and his girlfriend, Judy, had ridden their BMW motorcycles across country and through Canada out to San Francisco to get a job at the Exploratorium. When he put his mind to it, he would succeed, and there he was. They got an apartment nearby in the Marina and became friends with Frankie and Mimi. It wasn't long before they were over at Frankie's house doing all-nighters, listening to "Sail Away," playing chess. They were bright and funny, with that "syrup-sucking stump-jumper" sense of humor, like everybody in Vermont.

As good as he had it, Frankie wanted to make a go at having his own shop, one he could share with Robert and Gordon. It was raining the day they drove into Pier 40 and parked. "Let's get out and look around," said Frankie. They came to an open door of one of the bays to see a guy with long hair and thick glasses. He saw them and said, "Hi, come on in. What can I do for you?" The shop was turned into a display for the backgammon board and chess board tables he made there and was selling them. "Nice, you made these?" asked Robert.

"Yeah, thank you," he said.

"You guys looking for some space? I'm looking for someone to share this one with," he said. Frankie, Robert, and Gordon all looked at each other. "Half of this fifteen hundred-square-foot space, a hundred and fifty," he said.

"I'm Frankie. This is Robert and Gordon." They all shook.

"I'm Tony Caliban," he said.

"What about tools? Got a table saw?"

"Right over there. I don't have everything, but a lot of good stuff," said Tony.

"We have tools. Let's get this thing started this weekend," said Frankie. He had no intention of leaving the museum. He would do both. The Palace of Fine Arts was not far from Pier 40, it took 15 minutes in those days. Robert was stuck in the back of the dusty dysfunctional Coop, and Gordon wasn't doing anything that important and could always go back to what he was doing if it didn't work out. The big loading doors opened out onto the pier, so there was that space to work, not to mention it was incredibly beautiful and just a great place to hang out.

Frankie knew Malie liked hanging out with Robert and Gordon and was going to be part of the deal as far as Frankie was concerned. He would, of course, stay at the Coop; he carried the place on his back, but he had enough to do it all. "I'm going down to pier 40 tomorrow, wanna go?" Frankie asked Malie.

He knew what was happening and said, "Oh, yeah, Frankie, I help you."

Frankie bought a half-ton '54 F-100 pickup unfinished hot rod from the boyfriend of the guy's daughter who owned the little country store across the street from Frankie, Bob. He was a hillbilly in the heart of San Francisco. Nothing really unusual about that; there were hillbillies everywhere. Bob's daughter attracted one and had the truck for sale—a seriously hot-rodded Mercury 312 T Bird engine, with four barrel carbs glass packs, four-speed Hurst linkage, and chrome running boards and tailgate. The guy was not just a dumb hick; he was an artist too. He made a horn 6 or 8 that he put on top, a couple of redwood handles, and bed panels. With every panel, he used a different color primer; it was cool. You got out of the way if you saw it coming. It got the name Okie's Wet Dream.

They got Ray, an art teacher right up the hill from Frankie, from the Coop, with the nicest sixteen-inch table saw, which was sitting in his garage, to contribute by loaning the new shop the saw. Tony bought a blade for the saw. Malie built wood racks. Tables were built, lights were hung, and a woodshop took shape. They had laughs doing it, as always.

The sun was shining into the shop through the large roll-up doors that opened up to the pier and the water of the bay. A tug, a trimaran, and a couple of minesweepers tied up along the pier shared by everyone who had a space, one of many were on the pier. They could see up and down the pier that others with small woodworking operations were out in the sun.

At the front of the pier, upstairs was, yep, the Ant Farm, those crazy boys and their art. No telling what they were up to, but Frankie looked up there (an upstairs office looking out on the roadway), the Embarcadero. He didn't hear anything because the media finally figured out that the joke was on them, so they didn't show up for the moment of impact anymore. Across from them, in the other office, looking out in front, yep, Coyote. Call Off Your Old Tired Ethics. Never did see Margo either. She was getting it somewhere, not there.

Bruce Sprule had a woodshop and a stripping and refinishing operation in a ground floor shop under the Ant Farm and a pool table in a dark room, with beer, music, and pot. They ended up there a lot. He was actually a drug dealer too. Pot. Had nice cars and a nice place in Santa Cruz. He liked coke like everyone else.

The real action was at Billy's shop, next to theirs. He turned his entire shop into a slot car track. Another one.

"Tony, wanna toot?" Frankie finally asked him.

"I was wondering when you were going to ask," he said.

"How'd you know we did coke?" said Frankie.

"You could say I have a nose for it," he said. Snorting coke and racing slot cars became a favorite pastime for the guys in the shop and whoever else showed up. Bruce came down when he heard the fun and joined in. Then there was Death Frisbee. Death Frisbee was a game of throwing circular saw blades into big chunks of wood without getting stuck by the blades when they didn't stick and came flying back toward the thrower.

The guys who had the lease on the pier from the port had a camper shell business in pier 32 under the Bay Bridge and needed someone (Robert and Gordon) to build carpet kits for truck owners who were buying shells. A carpet kit was carpet-covered boxes that went over the wheel wells in the bed and elevated the bed up to provide storage below a platform on which to sleep.

They were selling like hotcakes, and they were actually bringing money in. If death frisbee and slot car racing didn't satisfy your need to screw around when there was work to be done, Tony bought a kayak. Robert was the first to fall in the icy bay out of the thing, then it was Frankie's turn. He was underneath the dark pier paddling along and had been lucky to have missed the pilings by the fact the paddle was diagonal and cleared. When he reached the innermost part of the pier, he was holding the paddle (over eight feet long with a flat paddle at each end) horizontally. The paddle hit the pilings and wiped Frankie out of the kayak and into the icy water, fully clothed. Thrashing around, he was barely able to pull the kayak (which was full of water) and the paddle to the platform, where the laughing group of smart alecks helped him out of the water.

It was time for Frankie to upgrade his image more and decided to buy a "bomber." He found a '53 Olds Rocket 88, four-door sedan. He had to borrow some money from Marguirette. It was off white with a green and cherry top. Inside was mohair and cashmere about the size of a living room. He was styling now.

Kevin helped him fabricate a false inside of the glove box, which was huge, and in the middle of the dash to cover up the blue glass plate for snorting coke off. Bill Parker made a long glass tube that clipped inside the cover next to the plate. The false cover unclipped so lines could be made for those in the back seat.

Took would come over once in a while and cook for Frankie and Mimi. He liked the part where Frankie stuffed generous amounts of coke up his nose after dinner, which was always four stars. He read palms and was a bit of a mystic, so he talked spiritual path while tossing the scampi.

"I was coming over here on the bus, and some youngsters were asking me what was in the bag," he said. "They said, 'let's see, mista.' I had to get up, go over, look at him, and say, 'None of your business, boy, *comprende*?' He got the message," he said.

"Well, of course, Took, you're a big nigger," said Frankie. Took sort of gave Frankie a blank look, not getting that Frankie meant the "way you were perceived" rather than calling him a nigger. It was not talked about, and Took never came over to cook again.

Frankie would borrow Kevin's Mini Cooper to zip over to pier 40 from the museum. Kevin got one after they saw the original *The Italian Job* with Michael Caine. They stole a load of gold from central Rome and used three Minis to transport it out of the city through sewer pipes, up and down stairs, places no other cars could go. Frankie drove it like that through the Marina, Fort Mason, Fisherman's Wharf, the Embarcadero.

Bobby, formerly neighbor from Plain Dealing, who got Frankie the gig at the museum and sold him some great pot, was living in New Orleans doing property development. He was buying properties, remodeling them, renting them, or selling them, making a tidy profit. He invited them to Mardi Gras. People who lived in New Orleans normally left town during Mardi Gras, but he was stuck there working on one of his ventures.

In the spirit of *Fear and Loathing in Las Vegas* by Hunter S. Thompson, they blasted off with plenty of drugs and a pocket full of money. The Camaro did 130 with no problem, and Frankie was in Arizona before he knew it. With the first hint of light, the state troopers hid in predictable spots, and Frankie was hip to their ways and slowed sufficiently to not get a ticket. Route 66 was a source of revenue for the counties along the highway; they were getting payment on the spot from out-of-staters exceeding the speed limit. It was otherwise a blur; they made it to New Orleans in two days.

"Frankie, Mimi, how was your trip?" asked Bobby when they finally found his very nice middle-class house in the upscale residential New Orleans neighborhood.

"Pretty frazzled, but we made it." Bobby showed them their quarters and let them shower and retire, which they needed. They rose the next day.

Karen was up to fix them breakfast. "Bobby's working today, so I'm in charge of giving you the tour," she said. They finished a wonderful breakfast and well groomed, got into the Mercedes, and headed to the French Quarter. They walked around with smoking hot Karen, who, being from "New Aleans," was a good guide and knew her local history. They spent the day there and at four got the dime-for-a-dozen oysters on the half shell on a white marble bar as old as the Civil War on Bourbon Street and bought a T-shirt.

Time to get back to the house so they could hook up with Bobby for the Fat Tuesday beginning of the celebration that night.

"This is my friend, Roger," said Bobby, and a large Southern-looking fellow stuck out his hand.

"Pleased to meet you," Roger said and shook hands.

"This is Mimi, my girlfriend," said Frankie.

"My pleasure, how ya doin', darlin?" said Roger.

"Roger knows the right people to get us a spot on the balcony over the heart of the parade. He's a bodyguard for a judge here in town," said Bobby. "He knows the right people."

Roger drove his big white Lincoln with everybody in the back and showed them where so and so lived and what he had to do to a guy in that place. "I had to hit the nigger in the kidney right here—undetectable, doesn't leave a mark—so hard his whole family was walking like this." He bent over in a contorted-looking way.

"I'd have to kill you if you did that to me," said Frankie, the good liberal down here in the South. Equal rights for black people.

"It's different down here, Frankie," said Bobby. No need to put the party in the dumper before they got there.

From the balcony of the beautifully appointed cat house, they yelled, "Hey, mister, throw me some beads." The guys on the floats were krewes and obliged by throwing beads at the people. Each krewe was a secret society, and no one knew their identities; they were completely covered with masks that even covered the back of their heads. Sinister in their adornments but generous with their beads.

They drank a lot, snorted a lot, and had their fill. Time for another eight ball and back to Bobby's. Big Bad Roger kept talking about "whole families of niggers walking like this." He revealed how corrupt the judge was for whom he was bodyguard. He snorted coke and sentenced blacks for long terms for getting caught with it.

He was all tied up in all kinds of shady activities but was above reproach, and he even had a long braided ponytail. When he could get a word in to voice his displeasure, Frankie had to keep a lid on it. Roger was a big, mean dude, couldn't piss him off too much. They were in his house.

A bit more Mardi Gras and then recovery from it, and Bobby found time to give a more thorough tour—the Super Dome, LSU, and all the other meaningful sites.

They had a blast, and it was time to go home. They took the more northern route and took their time. In Northern New Mexico, they ran across some Navajo jewelry they had to have, but the money was gone. The mother of pearl bracelet, for Frankie, was beautiful and had to be sent COD. That worked.

Once home, Kim had literally watered the plants every day whether they needed it or not. He was well educated but had no common sense. The catch dishes under the pots were overflowing.

What an idiot. It turned out Kim, who was left there to take care of things, took advantage of the party pad at his disposal and had a party, as if it was his. He invited a bunch of people he didn't know, and some he did. Antonio did a flamenco dance on the kitchen floor over John's hovel below. John came up at three thirty in the morning to see what the fuck was going on. It broke up the party and made it clear to most people they were not supposed to be there. Frankie would meet people for years after that who would say, "I've been here before." Must have been a good party. Frankie heard it was.

The wave was lapping up on the beach; it was in town. The Stone on Broadway (the original on Broadway, before Voss Boreta had the Off Broadway) was a good club and had some bands. The Savoy Tivoli, on Grant Avenue, had a club in the back and was a good venue for bands like that. Noisy, raucous. But the real new venue for Punk rock was the Mabuhay Gardens on Broadway, a Filipino-Polynesian restaurant during the day, Punk rock venue at night. Dirk Dirksen was the proprietor, a nerdy gay guy who often got punched out by the angry punks but was a seer of things to come. He mistakenly spiked the gin and vodka with grain alcohol thinking it would sedate the savage beasts, but all it did was inflame a volatile situation already about to explode, and it often did; it was angry, it was Punk.

Frankie hung out there quite a bit/ King Kong and bands he knew played there. Punk was fun because just about anybody could pick up a guitar and start slamming out an angry tune and just about everybody and his brother did.

There were bands like the Sex Pistols. Sid Vicious was a good example of someone who didn't know how to play, but he beat on the thing with a snarl. The Ramones were actually playing CBGBs, first in New York. The Clash, The Jam, Velvet Underground. The great Iggy Pop had already been around for years, from Detroit, Iggy and The Stooges.

Tom, John's younger brother, was back from Peru and Bolivia. He wondered what he was doing down there. He was there for a couple of years. Must have had a difference of opinion about something that was none of Frankie's business. He didn't seem like he liked being there, but he was cool. He could beat John at chess, and

Frankie could beat Tom. He still couldn't beat John—maddening. John had Frankie psyched; that's all there was to it.

Tom, just back from the age of stone, was in for a shocker when Frankie and Mimi took him to see the opening of *Star Wars* at the Geary Theater. Frankie did some speed (he didn't know why, because he hated it) and was in a foul mood and slept through some of it. Figure that one. The part he did see he hated it and would've walked out.

Tom didn't let any of that bother him and was falling off his seat in amazement; he looked like a little kid getting tickled. He was a pleasant, enlightened dude with a smile for whomever he met. Frankie got him a job at the museum as a painter, which they needed. Jackie and Anabelle loved him.

Frankie and Antonio were at a party in Sausalito at a recording studio, and across the dance floor were a couple of hot broads looking their way. Frankie held up his hand and, using his index finger, signaled, "Come here." They walked over, and Frankie said, "Hi, I'm Frankie. This is Tony. What're your names?"

"Kathy and Madeline," said the tall attractive brunette. They danced to the new band, Blondie, "One Way or Another"—"I'm Going to Getcha, Getcha, Getcha."

"Wanna do a line?" asked Frankie.

"Okay," she said. They went out to Olivia, and while chopping out lines on the blue glass and on the tray for Antonio and Madeline in back, he asked, "So what do you do, Kathy?"

"I'm a men's clothing buyer for Macy's, just moved here from New York," she said.

"That's cool. So you travel all over, eh?" asked Frankie. They stuck close to these two and followed them home to Kathy's Marina apartment. Invited in, they got inside and into her bedroom. Frankie said, "So, can I stay here with you tonight?"

"I really like you, and I would say yes, but having sex kind of freaks me out. But I'd love to be friends. I need a friend," she said. He had not been turned down before and thought everybody else was sex crazed too. It was no problem that she was not like everybody else. Her girlfriends were a different story. They all wanted it hard, lucky for Frankie.

Year 1977, Jimmy Carter became president. There was good reason to smash things. He did pardon Vietnam War draft evaders, while all the countries that hated us were the only ones producing petroleum, and there was not enough, even though they asked them nicely. We had to drive 55; there was a gas shortage. He gave away the Panama Canal. Studio 54 opened in New York City. It celebrated the new drug of choice openly by snorting it on the dance floor, didn't even have to go to the bathroom. Elvis, the king of rock and roll, died on the toilet.

BBQ got a job driving a limo and would deliver Frankie to the Mabuhay. He would wear the most damaged motorcycle jacket (very Punk), hop out in front, and go in like a big shot. Mimi had her fun but didn't like that scene. She was home. Or she was more likely to come if he'd deliver them to the disco around the corner, on Montgomery. Two totally different worlds.

There was a contingent of Punk groupies who were available, if you didn't get too fucked up. Otherwise you could get in a fight. Bad behavior and rejection of everything that came before was what Punk was about. The culture had already rejected Nixon, Reagan, and the warmongering establishment; it was now rejecting what had replaced it. They just didn't know it. It rebelled against everything, and even the so-called New Wave was too commercial to be considered Punk. Who cares? So what! Well, a lot of people did.

The work on Pier 40 kept Robert and Gordon alive, work found its way to them. Robert drank a lot of Schlitzes, twelve a day, whew.

Gano was a large man with a cute French wife who had an import business of French furniture made in the Philippines and hung out with the boys a little bit. He had a space across from them which they took over when he moved to a different warehouse. He sold Frankie his Alfa 2600 Spyder with a Buick aluminum V8 to put in it. It was there, and he got it cheap, just had to put it in. Right. They had a lot more space and access to that side of the pier. Al Giddings had a research vessel parked right outside the door. Robert was a really bright guy and asked all the right questions of the divers, and Al had the space next door. He filmed a bunch of big-time scary great white shark feeding frenzies and had close-ups and some brave, or stupid, divers. They made plenty of money doing it.

One day Frankie zipped down there from the museum, and nobody was around; maybe it was early. Outside his bay were a couple of guys working off some scaffolding. "Hey, man, this is my shop. I don't have my keys, and I was wondering if you wouldn't mind climbing up there and getting what I need to get and begone, he said.

The dumb kid he had just empowered with control over someone like what his idiot Italian family had over him said, "No, no, you can't."

Defeated, Frankie retreated to the car to try to figure out what to do. The idiot kid went to piss or something, and Frankie ran up the scaffold over the wall, grabbed what he needed to grab, and went back over the wall. The piece of shit hit him in the eye and cold-cocked him with tinted glasses on, which broke and cut his eye. The cops got called, and being the Embarcadero, they were there in about a minute. They grabbed Frankie, who truly felt like killing the little shithead. There was a guy who had a space nearby, whom they kind of knew; he was probably the one to call the cops. A good nurturing son, who probably grew up in Seacliff, went to Hastings, working his way up in the district attorney's office, gave Frankie a hot cup of coffee, who had the opportunity to throw it directly into the motherfucker's eyes. He screamed like he blinded him but far from it. Frankie still wanted to kill the little asshole. A further melee broke out, and Frankie got arrested. At the police station, they cleaned him up and let him go, no charges. That's when the cops looked at what actually happened and did the right thing.

Another twisted character but extremely intelligent, pretty much of hick, from Placerville, Rick did exhibit maintenance and could fix anything. He was also a Deadhead and liked taking drugs too. The Okie's Wet Dream got a beautiful new three-inch steel front bumper that was to clear pedestrians who didn't have the sense to get the fuck out of the way or they'd be dead. Compliments of Rick, a true master with a twisted sense of humor.

Gano, from Pier 40, found out that the museum was the place to get the highly specialized welding and machining done on his very special Harley. There were Rick and David, who was another genius machinist at the museum and the people there and their affinity for motorcycles. Gano was lucky to get highly skilled people to make parts for his bike for free.

Billy from Marin had some reconstituted coke that everybody loved. Not that the effect of the drug was any better; in fact it wasn't what it was when it wasn't so cleaned up and was without the effects it once gave. The good stuff turned one into the idiot they wanted to be turned into. The thought that it was cleaned up appealed to everybody. Did they really want to get high in the first place? Maybe not. Not that they were any smarter, so they didn't know. Getting high was getting stupid. It sure didn't make one any smarter.

The reconstituted coke got them to thinking. They were scientists; why couldn't they do that? Well, they could. They gravitated to the biology lab where they were able to start trying to figure out how to do that. They first had to figure out what the coke looked like under the microscope and in the spectrograph, which measured the degree to which polarized light refracted when sent through the pure crystals, which they would manipulate to lay flat on a slide by dissolving it in a nontoxic solvent and letting it recrystallize. So they figured out how to clean it up and reconstitute it, losing quite a bit of volume. They were stumped by a product that had a melting point almost exactly the same as coke but wasn't coke. Those cagey chemists in Bolivia and Peru, probably Klaus Barbie, the Nazi, created a product that behaved like coke but wasn't. Working on it night after night, snorting their fair share, Ripley finally said, "Why don't we just make it ourselves?"

Parker just said, "Let's do it." They were already able to test it for purity, and that was important to know.

Frankie's job was to get a molecule kit and start working on the cocaine molecule. He went to the Brisbane Library, which surprisingly had The History of, among many other chemical compound books. Very useful. Rip and Bill poured through everything they could find on the subject and found that the base ingredient was econine. The Coca-Cola company became what it was today as a result of it being an elixir, a pick-me-up, gave you pep. It did that because the active ingredient was cocaine. The Harrison Act of 1915 prohibited it from being put into the soft drink. They knew it was dangerous, but hey, anything for a buck.

The Coca-Cola Company was required to take the econine out of the drink, but why not sell that to Merc Labs, who was licensed to make cocaine as an anesthetic legally, used in eye surgery. It was highly controlled by then and impossible to get. "Why don't we make it synthetically?" asked Frankie.

"It's complicated. There is no such thing as synthetic coke," said Bill, shaking his head in disappointment.

They figured out all they could do was to clean it up for resale. Were people Frankie knew paying more for an already expensive drug? Maybe not. It did give him the skills of testing the purity of coke, but those who bought it from him tested it too. It had to be clean and as cheap as they could get it, just like everything else. They wanted this and this and this, and it was going to cost how much? That was outrageous. They thought they were smart, but Frankie was smarter.

Frankie, Bill, and Ripley became good friends and hung out, got high, and had some laughs. They made some black T-shirts with the cocaine molecule printed on them in white notation on the front and said, "Science Is Wonderful."

Word of mouth was such that more and more business came his way. Many people wanted what Frankie had, to be in possession of something everybody wanted. More and more people wanted to know him, so they got the coke from him and sold it to their friends and made money.

One of these people was Pam, a graphic artist—pretty nice-looking, good job, well dressed, and somehow knew the gay community, whom she sold to. She hung around the bars in the Castro.

She had her shit together, bought an ounce a week. It was not like he asked for it, but on her own, she discovered shooting it was the way to get that high, that special high. She gave Frankie a new syringe (in the package). He figured, "What the hell. I can handle it."

Mimi was spending more time in Berkeley, and it didn't take long for Mark and Cybil to hit her up for a quarter ounce. They were hopeless, weak, and spoiled by somebody (Frankie had no idea who) and apparently figured enough time had gone by since his last beating. There was no way they could ask the people they knew who supplied them with coke who they owed money to. Frankie didn't really know any of this at the time. Not sure Mimi knew, but she was an easy target for them. Cybil being her younger sister, with nice cans, had the ability to get her way if she begged enough. And they sure needed some. They were so pathetic it wasn't funny.

Frankie gave in to get rid of them. Bad idea. They were so fucking stupid and needy, and now Frankie was too. He fronted them a quarter ounce.

After three days, they came out of hiding and showed up at Frankie's. In Mimi's room, Mark held up the baggie that had the original quarter ounce in it, he said. It clearly had been handled by him for those three days; the coke was gone and there was some kind of white very powdery powder, obviously not coke. "This shit's cut, look," he said.

"How could I give you another chance to fuck me? Obviously you snorted it and expect me to believe the baby powder or whatever it is you put in there is mine. Get the fuck out of here and get out now. You have one minute." After several minutes, he could hear Mark was in the same position he had been in for the better part of three days, holding up the bag, looking at it, fooling with it and how much it looked like, etc.

Frankie came in and said, "Your minute is up, out!" and pointed to the door again. Mark wanted to drag this shit on and on. Frankie had already beat the son of a bitch to a pulp once; he apparently didn't get the message. From his recollection of how New York Bob sliced up the redneck on Beacon Hill, not stabbing, he remembered "put your finger on the back of the blade and swipe back and forth. Draw some blood, scare them." Frankie pulled out his six-inch Buck and started drawing blood, Mark's blood.

They ran out the door, and Mark yelled, "I'm going to kill you, Frankie!"

Frankie thought, *Well, you know where I live, and thanks for the warning.* They went to the nearest hospital, Saint Luke's, and a cop came to the house. A big Irish cop, by himself. He rang the bell; when the door opened, he asked, "You Frankie Thomas?"

"Yeah," said Frankie.

"Let's go." He motioned to hurry up like they were going fishing. He didn't think about changing out the blood-spattered martial arts gi. Not much he could do about the tracks.

In the patrol car, the cop said, "What happened?"

"I've been coldcocked by that guy before and had to defend myself, and this time he would not get out of my house when I told him to leave, so I defended myself," said Frankie. It was true.

What Frankie learned was that there were some crazy people out there, but the effect of the drug was not good. People blamed the drug and took no responsibility for their behavior. It did turn people into monsters, no question about it.

"If you stick to that, you should be fine," said the cop.

A couple of days passed. Jail was gruesome. The angry blacks didn't like whitey much, and he got jumped by one of them while the eight or nine other black guys watched, thinking Frankie ratted them out. He had no idea what that might have been but got his own cell with the murderers and perverts that needed to be kept away from the general population. Mimi and Adriana came to visit and asked if he wanted them to bail him out. "No, I don't think they're going to charge me," he said.

"Okay," they said. The next day they let him out, no charges. Mark had given them so many conflicting stories and was such a piece-of-shit drug addict and wasn't hurt that bad. He couldn't get his story straight. The truth prevailed. The cops did notice the tracks on his arms, even though there was no physical evidence—not that they were looking what was going on at home.

Nancy, manager of the Exploratorium store, got a place in Ross that was a guest house to one of the many palatial mansions on Shady Lane. She needed a roommate, and Frankie encouraged Mimi to do it. She had a room with him and a perfect escape pad to go to where she would not be subject to the madness. She wasn't equipped to deal with the crazy street shit that actually happened in the dirty real world. And it could only get crazier.

Business was good. More and more people were getting on the bandwagon to hell. It made them overcome their inhibitions and talk and talk and talk and not make much sense, but no one was listening anyway; they were talking too.

Frankie was plenty preoccupied and not interested in what was going on at pier 40 when Gano called and said, "Have you seen the news?"

"No," said Frankie.

"Pier 40's on fire!" he said. Frankie hopped in the Okie's Wet Dream and screamed down there. Sure enough, it was on fire. The Ant Farm, it was suspected, was making something with an expanding two-part epoxy that was highly flammable and caught fire. Nothing anyone could do except watch it burn.

The fire burned the first half of the pier; they were able to save the outer half of the structures built on top of the pier. The pier itself was fine. All the units that had been built on it were what caught on fire and burned. It was a mess. Their belongings were gone. No more shop, no more Death Frisbee, no more slot car racing there, anyway. They helped Bruce move his stuff around. For some unknown reason, his shop didn't burn. Interesting, being he was below the Ant Farm. Gordon and Robert joined in with him to continue the not very lucrative business they had, but they liked the fun they had there. Frankie would visit for a game of pool or a pot deal with Bruce, who was never easy to do business with.

Frankie and Ripley did some "how much acid can we take?" trips to Frankie's favorite spot, Bass Lake, in Point Reyes. They would take up to a thousand mics of the broken sunglass squares, five hundred each. Or the other special edition from John Dean, white with red speckles, double-barreled, five hundred mics specially made for the experienced traveler.

There was, probably still is, a bay tree about two-thirds of the way to Bass Lake—the perfect spot to take a break in the lower branches, off the trail, a calm and tranquil place. They would take a break there and assess if they were stoned enough and usually decided they weren't and take more. Past Bass Lake was Pelican Lake, accessed only by the spillway (creek) at the west end into the ocean; otherwise, it was choked by reeds and cattails. Spring fed, incredibly beautiful. The birds loved it, no humans. Up from Pelican Lake was Fort Point. A trail went up to what was the high point, kind of a lookout.

Fort Point was the highest point, and at the top was where they would get that protection they needed. Protection from what wasn't clear, and it would emerge from it (the pit) like gods. They were masters of the universe descending down the protruding hill, getting to the crossroads of the trail to the beach and back to civilization at the edge of Pelican Lake. One time, Ripley found a wedding band that obviously a distraught lover had taken off at the beautiful vantage point with the view of the ocean below, a coastal spring-fed lake, and coastal mountains above, and cast it on the ground. The romance or marriage was over, to the happiness of Ripley, who found the ring, gold with a diamond, and put it on his finger.

Fortunately, the massive doses they took affected them a little differently. When Frankie was reduced to the babbling infant just outside of death, Ripley was cogent. He flippantly said, "Frankie, what is the matter with you? We're here in the most beautiful place on earth, and you're somewhere else worrying about something a million miles away from here. Snap out of it!" Whatever that meant.

Frankie ran like a horse up the trail and cleansed himself of the poisons and toxins he let into his soul. More accurately, he invited them into his soul; he deserved no gentle treatment. About the time Frankie came to terms with his destiny to that point and was able to remember who he was, Ripley would start seeing ambulances and crying family members. Frankie would turn the tables on him and give him the tough love treatment. They stripped down and went swimming in Bass Lake, so nice. They'd make the three-mile or so trek back to the parking lot. There was no hurry now. They overloaded the circuitry, blew it out, and it magically returned in perfect working order. They accepted, in the feeble world they inhabited, that change had to start from within. They rebooted their minds.

Kathy, even though frigid, liked coke and liked hanging out with Frankie. He never pushed her to have sex; her girlfriends were available for that. He was fine with not having to think he had to have sex with every broad he met. He was, in the truest sense of the word, liberated. He not only didn't feel the need to conquer, he would protect her from the savage beasts that felt they had to.

Frankie was a businessman, albeit a drug dealer, and needed assistance from resourceful people, like Adrianna. She worked downtown, and going home to Robert, who was transfixed on his latest sculpted piece in his studio in Brisbane, was not as entertaining as stopping at Frankie's and seeing what was happening. Something usually was. She'd bring a bottle of brandy.

They were having a drink, listening to a Stones record in the living room, and the doorbell rang. He looked down the stairs to the front door, and through the glass he was able to see a couple of dark figures. Even though he told everyone to call before they came by, they didn't; he was used to people coming by unannounced. He buzzed them in.

Up the stairs charged two gun-wielding black guys shouting, "Police, get down! Police, get down!" Frankie looked in amazement as the angry black guy hit him in the head with his gun and kicked him until he went down on the hallway floor.

"Where's the money? Give me the money, motherfucker!" said the black guy. He hit Frankie in the face with his nine-millimeter. Adrianna got dragged into the living room at gunpoint by the other black guy and said nothing. "Where's the money, motherfucker?" said the black guy. Frankie did have some cash in his bedroom in his bureau. "Move it. Where's the drugs?" said the black guy.

"Give him whatever he wants," said Adrianna from the other room. Frankie could hear the other black guy with a gun to Adrianna's head raping her, and she was so scared she couldn't or didn't want to make noise for fear of Frankie's fate. The black guy pushed Frankie into the kitchen, right past the ladder located in the hall closet going up into the attic, where the real money and drugs were.

"On the floor, motherfucker, on the floor." Frankie really didn't want to do that and stood. Standing, it became obvious he was bigger than the little cowardly armed robber. Without a gun, he would have been beaten by the bigger man, Frankie. He hit him with his pistol until he knocked him to his knees. He'd done this before. The black guy was angry because Frankie wasn't really resisting but not cooperating. On his knees, looking down at the floor, the guy put the gun on the top of Frankie's head and fired a shot. The blood started flowing; Frankie didn't even look at the guy and got up, ran to the back door, fully expecting to be shot dead but was going to die getting the fuck away. The guy must have thought the bullet entered Frankie's head, as did Frankie. Expecting to get shot in the back, he leaped out the back over the steps and broke his ankle when he landed on about the third step.

They split. Adrianna got raped, and Frankie had a broken ankle and got ripped off for a couple of thousand dollars. They were lucky.

It turned out, seemingly, that it was a black guy he knew—Phenas, a black Muslim of some kind, Frankie didn't know anything about that. Frankie treated him like a friend. He belonged to this group that hated white people; they were the devil. Frankie's mistake was to be totally generous to the guy, stuff lots of coke up his nose, and invite him along to the great parties. He gave free food, free drinks and was just being a friend. His crime was being white. He deserved to be destroyed. He not only tipped off the two cowardly armed robbers but gave them the layout of the place. They clearly knew he had money, drugs, nice-looking women around.

Panhandle Pete and John Dean both loaned $1,000 each to keep him afloat.

Frankie always got the best coke from Donnie, of Good Karma fame. He was a spiritualist and never touched the stuff himself. He was ahead of the curve, taking full advantage of the new epidemic to get rich. His obsession was not doing it. It wasn't hard to not do it. All one had to do was look around at what was happening. It wasn't good.

Susie White was a cute big-titted blonde from Daly City who came up to Frankie at the Mab and put her arm through his and said, "I'm going home with you." She was hot and knew it.

Frankie said, "Okay."

On the scene, she slept with many guys, and Frankie slept with a lot of local sluts too. It wasn't a big deal, and it wasn't; it was sex. The sex was routine, not earth-shattering. Not a big deal. She was cute; he liked her. He recalled Robert having said, "They all look the same from the bottom." When Frankie passed that on to Suzie in conversation, she said, "No, they don't." Robert was wrong. She was right, see.

Panhandle Pete introduced Frankie to Bart. Bart was the owner of Berkeley Square. They had money and dumped a bunch of it in the place to be the new venue for Punk rock and maybe even new wave.

Frankie would hang around with Rick, the hick from Placerville, at the museum. They had fun; he liked to work at night too. Not that they were doing museum work. The guy was really smart but whacko, and apparently, when Frankie jammed too much coke up his nose, which of course he totally resisted, he snapped. He gave Rick a ride home to his bad pad in Ghirardelli Square. It was somehow Frankie's fault that he had demons. He told stories of going for a walk in the woods with his mother and a shovel and only coming back with the shovel.

"I'll take a 2×4 to your head," he said. He was taller but in no way meaner than Frankie, daring him to move in the middle of the shop a couple of days later. Rick knew it.

Charlie, head of biology, somehow heard, probably from Rick, that Frankie made $50,000 a year dealing coke and that his salary at the museum was a mere pittance, which Frankie may have very well blabbed. The rumor got around, and the half of the staff who had been recipients of Frankie's generosity with coke could say they never believed it and the other half who weren't privy to it said, "That's terrible. We can't have that."

Frankie was livid about the backstabbing from Rick. It was Frankie's fault the sick motherfucker had demons and the coke he gave him revealed those demons. Frankie was starting to learn new things about the effects of the drug that were not within his control. People were fucked up. Frankie kept learning how much.

He got to the point that he realized that his fall from good standing at the museum was a result of these petty power-hungry figures with the power structure who would do anything and say anything to advance their agenda. That was politics; Frankie should have known that.

Frank called him at home and said, "Come on, Frankie. Come back. We don't care about that." "No" was all Frankie said. A dumb thing to say, never to be taken back. That would be the end of Frankie's association with the family that was the Exploratorium.

Tom, Mimi, Kevin, Pete, and Ripley would still have connections with Frankie. Larry, in graphics, and Frankie had plans before the breakup happened to go to LA—to watch the Long Beach Grand Prix, a great race of what's now IndyCars, then known as CART, with great drivers like Mario Andretti. They drove Larry's 2002 BMW down.

While in LA, he spent a bit of time with his friend and former roommate from Cambridge who was now doing a residency at LA General, Rickie. There was only so much time, but he did have a chance to make it to the Whiskey. It was the happening club on Sunset Boulevard.

He met a nice-looking blonde looking for a good time. They danced, and she took him home to her Beverly Hills apartment where he gave it to her good as far as he can remember. He didn't remember that much. She was good-looking but soft. That's about all he could remember. While at the car race, they were wandering around and came across a black Lamborghini with gold vents and grills all over with pieces of tumbleweed stuck in them, very dirty. It was clearly driven with disregard for the fact it was a hundred-thousand-dollar car. Empty Marlboro packs and fast-food wrappers were on the dash. It was parked in the loading zone right in front of the fanciest hotel in Long Beach, impressive.

Kathy knew professional people from New York, working in San Francisco, making money. Michael was a Pacific Exchange broker/trader working at First Boston or something like that, who wanted a gram here and a gram there. He had stock market friends who also wanted coke. Some were with Rolls-Royces, parked outside while they came in to cop. They just wanted it clean and would pay. They got to like him and would hang out and snort their coke— something new to Frankie.

With Mimi safely in Ross, the parade of pussy was at full march. Coke was the lure; likability and the new moral horizon lent itself to what Frankie was doing all along. The populous was coming around to the drug that had the effect they needed. Get over inhibitions, come out, talk a lot, and not make much sense. That group of clients was in.

He became well-known to the circle of stockbrokers, and some beyond the trade.

Glen was a guy somehow connected to Michael, the stockbroker. It must have been the interest in coke. Everybody wanted some. Glen was a television producer, black, well-groomed, and could make jokes about the social phenomena they took advantage of and made fun of. He was from Bedford Stuyvesant in Brooklyn and had a tough core but was charming and polished and loved coke.

He said, "So you're involved in Punk?"

"I am. Everyone hip is going that way."

"Interesting, I'd like to do a show about that," he said. The assistant or associate producer was Dennis Connery, son of Sean, or so he said. Sean denied any connection, and Dennis was gay. Not son of Sean. The job was primarily political and required the gift of gab. Dennis came with Glen when it came to scoring small amounts and was a hanger-on to the show business-related job. It didn't seem like he had any particular skills or good ideas.

Stock market Michael and Frankie did a couple of all-nighters sniffing large amounts of coke. He was on New York Stock Exchange time, so he had to be in his office in downtown San Francisco at 5:00 a.m. Must have been fun.

Frankie paid visits to Mimi in Ross, and if she wasn't in heels and a garter, they were lounging by the pool.

Tom was still at the museum but was also taking classes at City College. Frankie invited Tom to Brisbane to one of the many stargazing evenings they had looking through the telescope Frankie had purchased from Tom's older brother, John. Robert, Adrianna, Mimi, and Frankie would have a nice barbecue before it got dark enough and take some acid.

On this particular evening, Tom brought along his buddy from school, Hop. Hop was a Vietnam veteran from New York originally, prone to excess. He chugged a gallon of red wine before dinner and took acid. He passed out on the swing and spun quietly to a stop until he finally fell off under the swing. He was a load, about 250 pounds. Nobody moved him anywhere. The evening was over for everyone when he awoke and knew not where he was or who these people were. Nothing worse than waking up with a terrible hangover stoned on acid, but he was a jolly fellow; they laughed about it.

Father Tom, former director of Sanctuary, showed up in town and was visiting Marc and Mato, whom Frankie lived in Watertown with and worked at Sanctuary. They were going to San Francisco Art Institute and had a shitty little place (a rundown three-bedroom apartment) on Francisco Street just down from the college on Russian Hill. Frankie stopped by once in a while to get them high and have a cup of coffee, if it was before noon; otherwise, they drank bourbon and scotch, and they always had a beer.

They were artists. All sort of collage-type stuff caked with layers of crap held together by glue and paint and said. Who knows what it said?

Father Tom (he was, in fact, an ordained Episcopal priest) used his position in the church to do his art. He was checking it out and decided to come to SF and become a force of nature at the Art Institute.

Getting him acclimated, Frankie was doing what he usually did, jamming large amounts of coke up people's noses, and he did Tom's. He was not turning it down, but after a couple of days, he started to realize this was too much of a good thing. He warned him as non-judgmentally as he could. Frankie just did another line. He had it bad. The drug had taken him, as if it was the drug's fault.

Frankie could not get enough of the accolades that came with dealing coke. It was dangerous, yeah, but worth it. Everyone acted like you were the one who invented it and made them feel like they never did before, and Frankie was glad to take the credit. Just wait until they were strung out.

Hop was Tom's buddy, but he wanted to know more about dealing coke. He could lie on the couch and have bindles made up in his pocket, and people would come buy and he wouldn't even have to get up. And he didn't.

At the Mab, Frankie spotted a sultry little beauty who was out with friends and looking for a good time, but she was married—as if Frankie gave a shit. "Can I buy you and your friends a drink?" he asked.

"Yeah," she said. He could see the ring and the fact she was not getting the cock from her husband that her nineteen-year-old body asked for. And she had a kid, a young daughter. Sandy was, however, extremely sultry and sexy, and Frankie would get her. Later. Her friends, Julie and Ansel, were dirty and wanted some too. He'd get to them later. It turned out Julie's father owned the Saloon in Brisbane, where they also lived. How convenient. The Saloon was a bar where all the bikers and Hells Angels hung out.

Michael was fucking Dennis's girlfriend, Abby, at Frankie's a couple times a week. Dennis got wind of it but was under the impression Frankie was. He called Frankie and said, "I'm coming over there, and I'm going to kick your ass."

"Thanks for the warning. See you then," said Frankie. Since he was gay (maybe he didn't know it yet), it was not clear how he had a girlfriend, but he did, and he was jealous. There was no way he would have kicked anybody's ass, let alone a tough street kid bigger, smarter, and tougher than he would ever be. He had his .357 in hand when he let Dennis in, who charged up the stairs, and to Frankie's surprise, he started wrestling around with both Frankie and Michael—surprised he was so fearless or stupid. Without really realizing it, he knocked the gun out of Frankie's hand. It ended up on the floor for anyone to grab. Michael and Abby retreated into Mimi's unoccupied bedroom, where they had been fucking not too long before the excitement. Frankie got control of the gun and kicked Dennis down the stairs and said, "Get the fuck out of here before I blow your brains out," and pointed the gun at his head.

Abby was from a family of means, and her brother and some friends moved her stuff out of Dennis's Union Street apartment, including a big beautiful brass bed. That got stored, and Frankie let her stay at his place until she figured out what to do, which Michael was happy about. She was a nice-looking blonde. Frankie didn't even think about it; he was busy.

She stayed at Frankie's for a few days until Michael (a man of means) found her a place in Marin, where he could visit her every couple of days, away from his girlfriend at his place in Sausalito.

Glen heard the story, and that was it for Dennis. What an idiot.

"Want a job?" Glen asked Frankie.

Bayscene was a news-based human-interest TV magazine hosted by Jerry Jensen, the coanchor of the local ABC evening news, and Glen was the producer.

"So you know something about Punk rock, right?" he asked.

"Yeah," answered Frankie.

"Let's do a piece on that," he said.

"I'm interested," said Frankie. A perverted drug addict seemed to be his qualifications for the job, and Glen promptly hired him. Maybe the fact he was a coke dealer and Glen was very much a fan of coke had a little something to do with it.

As a producer, he didn't have to keep any kind of hours in the Circle Seven studio offices on Golden Gate Avenue, like everyone else did. He did take the job seriously, up all night thinking and writing about the subject of the new music. There was certainly enough material out there to take from for a good story, and with all the good contacts, like Bart, Berkeley Square, and Dirk, the Mabuhay, he had his finger on the pulse.

His buddy Stan had formed a group and called Gang Green and the Amputators. It was big-time wrestling meets Punk rock. The lead singer, Kenny something, usually chugged a fifth of vodka before going on stage. No apologies were ever given. As a producer of sorts, Frankie gave them advice on what to do next to get more people to listen to their music. They wore hopsack hoods, and Gang Green was almost naked, painted green and black. They completely ignored his advice. He knew the Tubes from the time they practiced at the Palace of Fine Arts theater. They were kind of Punk. They were before traditional Punk Rock but had their own prepunk song, "White Punks on Dope," and they were. They were more theatrical but outrageous and could be categorized as such. Fee Waybul, lead singer, was the most outrageous, hands down, than anything anybody had ever seen or ever will. Bless him; there will never be another. Bill Spooner was the lead guitarist and became a friend and connection, of his.

Bart, of course, owned Berkeley Square. All the important bands who played there were currently Punk. The place was painted pink and black, very Punk. Nice. But it was in Berkeley; they didn't know it, but they bowed to the groovy holier-than-thou edict and installed little negative ionization generators and hung them from the ceiling. They gave good energy, put you in a good mood, Berkeley. Every Punk wanted to play there.

"I'm planning to make a documentary film about Punk Rock. What do you think? Be interested in doing that with me?" Frankie said to Bart.

"Yeah, for sure, that sounds great," he said. "Where do you want to do it?"

"I'm not sure yet, somewhere in the City," said Frankie. Even though Bart had the hot club in Berkeley, it wasn't big enough; he needed more space. Bart didn't take it personally.

Frankie found the perfect place to have the show. Cesar's Palace, on Mission Street, a former boxing venue, right near Frankie's place. Cesar was a nice Mexican guy, happy to have anybody rent his place. They could have the door; he would take the bar. Okay, no problem.

There was New Orleans Bobby's friend Charles, who was a stained-glass artist who made beautiful lamps and things, many of which were sold at Plain Dealing. He also had good coke. Jack Cassady, Jefferson Airplane, Starship, and Hot Tuna bassist, was a close friend of his and had formed his own new Punk band with Brian Marnell, front man. Brian was the real article—very talented and a true Punk. SVT had been playing around, so Frankie knew them already. He asked them to headline the show he was about to promote, produce, and film a documentary of. Staging a Punk rock concert hadn't really been done before.

Miss Justice was a band with a hot piece of ass lead singer—had lots of leather and studs, pretattooed, pierced. They were more heavy metal, but Frankie wanted to fuck her, so they got on the bill.

Romeo Void was a band Bart had an interest in, so they were invited to perform for the exposure they were going to get, and they had a hit. "I might like you better if we slept together, but something in your eyes tells me never. Never say never…" The female lead singer was kind of chubby, and so it was easy to see why they came up with those lyrics.

Then, of course, Gang Green and the Amputators. They had to be invited.

The script had to be written, and Frankie set out to do that. It would not be an easy thing since it had never been done before. Glen was not worried; he would edit the final version and was glad to have someone doing the work he was responsible for. Not to mention everybody had an opinion what exactly defined the new music. It had its purists. If you sold out to make money, it was new wave. Mainstream. Not pure anymore. A view left over from the purity of what was hip and what wasn't. It's not like anybody realized any of that at the time.

New Wave or No Wave—it had a name.

Panhandle Pete was off to New York again and left his Jeep Wagoneer in Frankie's care, giving Frankie the perfect opportunity to take a trip to the mountains for a little rest and relaxation—to clean up actually.

His buddy Tom, who was at the museum and City College, had some Canadian friends in town, heh, and it seemed like a good idea to take them on a camping trip to the Sierras.

They were able to access a fairly remote mountain lake with the Jeep to do some fishing and just hanging out for a few days. Not enough to really get clean but with no drugs or alcohol, it was necessary to at least let the healing start.

Far from really healed, he returned to the City to get to work.

Not only was the show planned to stage a view of the new phenomena, it was planned to capture the fun and out-of-control nature the rowdy new form of music had. It was a happening scene, and Frankie was right there with an occupation that gave it credence and fueled its existence, cocaine.

Miss Justice was calling, looking for some cock and some coke. He only had to clean some sifting devices to get back to that jacked-up state, back to normal.

He took an ABC camera crew to the Mab to interview Dirk one morning. He learned that day the camera crew were a bunch of alcoholics also, so getting a couple drinks to get right was welcome before any footage got shot. Dirk was the usual bore and hadn't gotten right yet, so the interview was not insightful. He got asked the important questions: "What is Punk? Why is it so popular? Why do you have it here?" The guy was an empty vessel; he didn't know. It was never clear to Frankie how and why this guy ever got involved in this music scene. He himself wasn't Punk; he was a nerd, always getting beat up by some out of control little shithead who would get arrested, but it never looked good for him. Maybe that was it. He was gay, maybe a masochist who liked getting beaten up. That was the only thing that made sense. But as "The Pope of Punk," he had to be interviewed.

He interviewed Steven Kapan, the morning funny man at KSAN. This guy was the first shock jock. Everyone stole this guy's routine, everyone. This guy was hilarious and natural, really funny.

Frankie chose to interview him because of all that to ask him inane questions about Punk Rock, which, what did he know or care? Nothing.

He got to the station during his morning show, having done an all-nighter, walked in the live studio, and threw his last record like a Frisbee to Frankie.

The interview, though fun, didn't say much. "What does Punk mean to you?" asked Frankie.

"Just what it says, Punk," he said. How enlightening. Not that he was an authority or even cared about that. Panhandle Pete had introduced Frankie—or was it Bart?—to Peter. Peter was a guy who took the new music to its highest form of rebellion in the Berkeley tradition and also embraced Nazism. That'll show them what being radical is. He did have an interest in the band X, which was Punk, and had a couple records. They had legitimate Punk standing.

He had a naughty little Punk wife whom he had working hard making pleated little Irish skirts that go to market somewhere. This guy, Peter, didn't do anything that didn't make him money. Panhandle Pete probably didn't know how seriously he took the drug dealing, which was one of pride. He also took the Nazi part as a way of doing business into the scheme of things and was a ruthless, nasty fellow, living the Punk lifestyle.

The wife, who had a permanent snarl and like her husband who had taken rock and roll to a whole new level, like killing people if they didn't come around to their way of thinking, gave an interview. She gave an interview, saying, "If you're Punk, you're not selling out. If you're making money, you're New Wave. New Wave is not Punk."

He sought out a couple of people who wrote articles about the subject, "Punk Journalists." New Wave had "the slick patina of respectability," one said.

Frankie didn't like the guy, but he did have a great source of coke from South America imported and allegedly manufactured by Klaus Barbie, the Nazi, who successfully escaped Germany after the war from prosecution for war crimes. In Argentina was where many Nazis escaped to. Some think Hitler himself did—Peter's hero.

The coke came in small cylinders a little bigger than a stick of chalk and hence the name chalk, unable to be cut. It was killer, as only Germans could produce.

Donny, of Good Karma fame, was not only a great restauranteur and had great drug connections, he was also a very good photographer. He had a really good collection of pictures from a shoot of a nasty college girl with pointy Lucille Ball glasses. She had old-school sunglasses on, was topless (he just wanted to see her tits, like everybody with a pulse did), had her hair up kind of zigged and zagged over her head, hockey protective gear around her shoulders, and her nipples almost but not covered. In her hands were several round discs of Afghani hash in the almost exact shape of a hockey puck. So that's what they were called. It looked dangerous. With her luscious titties hanging out, she got selected for the poster for the event. She had that look of knowing that her boyfriend was going to give it to her hard when she got home, and Frankie got a boner just looking at it.

Pamela, Frankie's loyal customer and graphic artist, put together the poster for the boys, making it an object of art in the tradition of the Family Dog, the Avalon Ballroom, and Winterland.

She desperately wanted to fuck Frankie and got her wish, completing the process, and Frankie realized what a nasty bitch she was when she asked to be "tied up and fucked in the ass," which he was happy to do.

Even though Bart was supposed to be a partner in the event, Frankie did most of the work. They did do an interview at SF State College radio station and got asked all the usual questions. "What is Punk? What is your reason for showcasing it? Why so angry? Can I get tickets?" asked the disc jockey in training at the school.

Bart did have connections through owning the Berkeley Square, such as Tumbleweed, the sound guy. They paid some guys to go to North Beach and to other clubs to pass out small posters for the upcoming event. Frankie even forked over $800 to have KSAN produce and run a commercial for the event. They were going to preserve Punk's noncommercial integrity but let everyone know it was going to happen. There were a lot of people hungry for something new; they were tired of regular old mainstream rock. The stage was set.

Mimi and Adrianna were at the door. Malie sat on a stool near the door and took a close look at everybody who came in. Brother Dana showed up with a friend from the Navy. "Hey, Dana, could you give Malie a hand with the door?"

"Malie doesn't look like he needs any help with the door," he said, with eyes wide. Frankie knew he was right about that.

Cezar was as happy as a greedy little Mexican could be. He was at the cash register in the middle of the large circular island bar that had people standing two deep, waiting for a drink, before the music started. The punkette from KUSF who interviewed Bart was there, and Frankie was DJ and played records she brought at intermission, digging it.

Glen and the ABC Bayscene camera crew did the interviews with punked-out-looking kids, as well as a couple of preshow interviews with band members in dressing rooms.

He set up an interview with Chet, who was respected and maybe knew something about music. He had an opinion.

"What is the difference between Punk Rock and New Wave?" asked Frankie.

"Well, New Wave is much more inclusive," he said. Like everything, there was no social agreement on what was what. They all had an opinion. It wasn't but ten years prior the Berkeley elite said, "Don't trust anybody over thirty-five." Now they were thirty-five. Oops.

They, the Berkeley elite, had fashioned an authority that demonized anything that didn't fit into their plan for the future for them to control everything, especially what one thought.

People from the past, like New York Dan, looking the same, with the same black velvet cape, (too old for Punk) were on the lookout for pussy. When he saw Frankie at the door, who was clearly running the show, he said, "Frankie, are you doing this show? Let me in free!"

"Dan, look at you. You haven't changed a bit, have you? Dan, it's six bucks. If I let everyone I know in for free, I'd go broke. Can't do it."

"Frankie, all the things I've done for you over the years," he said.

"Okay, go, go," he said and waved him in. Malie could see what was happening and could have killed him, but he just gave a look to let him know that fact. He didn't like his Clyde Crashcup demeanor.

Gang Green and the Amputators played first. Kenny, the lead singer, was almost naked, painted green, and was drunk, while Stan, who played lead guitar, the bass player, and the drummer (Paul, the biker) had on gunny sacks and pointed black hoods. Stan's guitar was a big sharp-looking ax. The crowd was blown away; a few clapped. Most just looked at them in awe and were glad the screeching was over. Frankie was glad that was over with.

Bart had some sort of financial interest in Romeo Void, so he introduced them as Master of Ceremonies. Frankie was in Miss Justice's dressing room packing his and her noses.

"People, you're going to love this band if you don't already," said Frankie to the audience, looking right at her behind the amps waiting to run out and start performing. "Meet Miss Justice!" he said and grabbed her affectionately as they passed. They were a heavy metal band that wore lots of studded black leather. Miss Justice's theme was guns, bullets, injustice, getting even, or something. The important thing was that she had a great ass. He would get to that, but they weren't really Punk, but close enough.

Glen and the camera crew were getting plenty of good footage, but they were also interested in drinking and did plenty of that too. They were not privy to the fact Glen and Frankie were doing coke and had to be discreet about it.

Bart beat Frankie to the punch when SVT was ready to go on and ran out onstage and grabbed the microphone and said, "Okay, everybody, they're here, SVT." They were the band everybody was there to see and applauded loudly. Brian Marnell was very talented and looked the part. He had natural spikey black hair and wore a long-sleeved (to hide tracks) white shirt out of the hamper, wrinkled and partly buttoned. "Heart of Stone" was what he wrote; not the Stones version, they played first. "Down, Down, Down, into a Burning Ring of Fire, Flames got Higher." This blew everyone away. Smart of Jack to be the one to put him up there; they were great.

Frankie was near the bar, and up to him came Antonio's girlfriend Milly. She said, "Great show, Frankie, I'm having a good time."

"Oh hello, I'm glad you are. My, don't you look like a Greek goddess."

"How nice of you to say," she said. Nobody mentioned that Antonio was in Amsterdam introducing them to MDMA, fucking Dutch, French, and Spanish broads.

She was a mature blond beauty elegantly attired in some sort of tightly wrapped satin pants and a top that brought out the fact she had a smoking hot body.

"Buy you a drink?" he asked.

"Love one," she said.

He made a gesture to Cesar with his finger, and observing the sight, he smiled and said, "What can I get you, Mr. Frankie?"

He looked at Milly. "Bourbon," she said.

"I'll have one too, Cesar. Thanks. So what do you do, Milly?" he asked.

"I'm a model and a writer," she said.

"A writer? You're not an alcoholic, are you?"

"No, I'm not an alcoholic," she said, seeming to get the message, the message being many of the great writers were stoned alcoholics; it was well-known. Any literary student would know that.

"So you promote or somehow make these things happen?"

"I'm doing this one to film and make a documentary about it. It's what's new. I'm hanging on to the edge of it, yeah. It's interesting."

Glen came up. "The crew is rolled up and in the van. It's a wrap. Can I speak to you for a minute?"

"Of course, be right back," he said. He introduced the two. "Milly, Glen."

"My pleasure." He, of course, wanted some coke, a gram. Frankie went outside with Glen, who said, "Who is that?"

"A lady I know through a mutual friend, who's away at the moment," said Frankie.

"Lucky you," he said. Frankie gave him his bindle and went in to see if she was still there. She was. "So why don't we have lunch sometime this week?" he said.

"Why don't you come over and I'll make you lunch?" she said.

"I'll call you on Wednesday," he said as she handed him her number.

The show was a success. The DJ spun records until well after 2:00 a.m., and Cesar was serving drinks until well after 3:00 a.m. when Frankie and his friends helped him go back to his place to count the money they made. It turned out Bart was very generous with Frankie's money by letting a lot of his friends (and New York Dan) in for free. He came up short. It cost him about $1,500. Good thing he had the lucrative drug business to pay for it. He blew it off and invited everyone to the Geneva Bowl, where they took over about three lanes at the end and were served drinks and did lines of the scoring tables and bowled.

Frankie somehow didn't get the word, probably because it was a last minute-thing and he was incommunicado in the attic preoccupied with some vixen's inner workings, but in 1978, The Sex Pistols played their last show at Winterland. The Bee Gees came out with *Saturday Night Fever*, and even though a true Punk hated that scene (and everything that wasn't Punk), Frankie still liked the scene even though he could surely do without John Travolta and the way he was portrayed in the movie. Frankie's blood-soaked white suit was ruined anyway. He was wearing that to the clubs way before the stupid movie. Roman

Polanski pleaded guilty to having sex with a thirteen-year-old girl and skipped bail to France, where they would never send him back. Hustler publisher Larry Flint was shot in Georgia by a sniper and became crippled. Every country on the planet was setting off nukes at an alarming rate. Testing, they called it. But of course, it was flexing their muscles, trying to impress their cold war opponents, including France. Who could give a shit if France had a nuclear bomb, but by now, the entire South Pacific was glowing from their many tests. Fallout was drifting to Australia, who was about to declare war on the stupid frogs for doing so. The whacked-out Unification Church drew a lot of attention by having multiple and then mass weddings. It was the first visible cult of its kind. The followers were seemingly brainwashed by their leader. The Police played for the first time in the US at CBGBs in New York City. They were interesting, but soon enough what really caught Frankie's ear was the underground artist by the name of Klark Kent. It was Stuart Copeland, drummer for the Police, even though he denied it. He wore a bag over his head when he did an interview.

Wednesday morning, well rested and recovered from the show, he called Milly. She had lunch planned for whenever he arrived. She lived about five blocks away. He arrived with flowers and a bottle of champagne. "Oh, don't you look lovely," he said. She did when she opened the door. He handed her the flowers. "Oh, aren't these nice. Thank you," she said and took the flowers. "Come in. Sit down, I'll get lunch." She walked into the kitchen as Frankie sat down in the dining room. Next to the dining room, the living room was beautifully furnished with overstuffed chairs, floral-printed fabrics and curtains, lace shades on the lamps—very feminine. In the spacious, elegant apartment, he could see into the bedroom through the double glass-paned doors that the bed was turned down, ready to get in between the sheets, similarly floral prints with comfy pillows. She came in with the flowers in a vase and two champagne glasses and said, "I hope you like seafood. I made paella."

Even though he wasn't quite sure what that was, he said, "Sounds good." He popped the champagne skillfully, not spilling a drop, and poured it into the two glasses. They tipped glasses and stared at one another knowingly and drank.

Gazing at each other eating Paella at the dinner table, Frankie said, "What kind of modeling do you do?"

"I model clothing, and I'm an artist's model," she said.

"Artist's model?" said Frankie.

"Yeah, nude modeling for art classes, figure drawing, that kind of thing," she said.

"You're obviously a gourmet cook too. This Paella is delicious," he said.

"I'm glad you like it," she said. With a mussel in his spoon that looked just like a vagina, he looked at it then looked up at her and said, "I love it," and ate the mussel and smiled. She took the dishes to the sink and was cleaning up when he brought his plate in and couldn't help but put his arms around her and start kissing her neck. She went, "Oh yeah," and he moved his hands to her delicious large breasts and began caressing them for a while. She turned and led him by the hand down the hall and into the bedroom. They got undressed and into bed, and he, in the traditional way, climbed on top, spread her legs, and stuck his very hard cock into her very wet pussy.

They made love madly for a couple of minutes, and in mutual orgasm they clenched each other by the mouths and moaned in unison. It took about five minutes. Frankie rolled off and said, "Oh, Milly," of course. She smiled and put her arm around him and kissed his face. She got up and closed the curtains in the bedroom, got back into bed, and they napped.

It felt like it was the right way to live. From there, they went back to Frankie's place, where the phone was ringing off the hook for drugs, of course.

They moved into the attic for the evening and started snorting coke while the parade of people needing coke came through. When he put an end to it, Frankie and Milly made love some more. She was a classy broad, so Frankie didn't get her in the sling right away. He'd take his time. Milly said, "I've got to get home. I have a photo shoot on the beach tomorrow."

"Okay, dear, see you." When he saw a picture from the photo shoot later, it was her naked and standing on the sunny beach with a large silk scarf blowing in the wind. She looked like the Greek goddess Venus.

Glen, luckily, had someone get footage of the Sex Pistols at Winterland, and there was still a lot of work to do on *New Wave or No Wave*. Kathy asked Frankie if he wanted to go to New York with her for a week. They could stay at her mother's Manhattan apartment and at her East Hampton house; it would be fun. It was only for a week or so. Glen said, "Of course, go to New York for a week. This will be here when you get back. Have a good time."

Michael, the stockbroker, brought over some crazy friends he did business with one of whom was Junior, a strawberry broker who lived half the year in Monterey and the other half in Florida. They were snorting coke and shooting the bow and arrows in the attic, and Junior said, "I'm leaving for Florida tomorrow. Come down and visit after you go to New York since you're out there. It'll be great. I have a condo in the same complex as the Pittsburg Pirates, at their winter camp. Come down and meet Willie Stargell. He loves coke. I know all kinds of hot girls who'll give you a blue veiner."

It sounded pretty inviting. Michael said, "Frankie, you gotta go. It sounds too good to pass up," and he was right. Of course he knew by now that he was very popular by the fact he always had coke and people jacked up having a good old time in his attic drinking and snorting said many things, but he said, "Yeah, sounds good. Tampa, huh. I'll fly down for a couple days."

John Dean lent him the coolest stainless-steel luggage, very expensive, that he bought when he went to France on the Concorde to use. He and Kathy were ready to leave.

"Milly, it's Frankie. How are you, my dear?"

"Good, and you?" she said.

"I'm going back east for a week or so. I'm going to miss you. I'll see you when I get back."

"I'm going to miss you too. I probably won't be here when you get back. Antonio's back from Amsterdam, and he wants me to take a trip to Paris next week. I won't be gone long, though, just a couple of days," she said. "See you when you get back. Goodbye."

"Goodbye." Frankie and Antonio were good friends, and it didn't bother either of them that he and Milly had an encounter. Frankie knew Tony wasn't the jealous type, having open relationships, especially since he was over in Amsterdam picking the fruit from the tree, liberally, himself.

He was so cool he not only never paid for it, it had to be free. The fact of the matter was that Milly spoke French and was carrying some grams of acid to a connection of his in a deal and coming right back. He wasn't even going with her; she was a mule—an attractive, professional woman on business. Frankie didn't know at the time; it didn't matter to him anyway either.

A couple of DC10s had just crashed, so people were afraid to fly them. They took a red-eye, and it was empty. Good for Frankie, he didn't have to be discreet when snorting coke and was completely jacked up by the time they got to New York, not to mention he had done an all-nighter the night before.

"Hi, Ma, how are you?" said to her sweet-looking Jewish mother who had come to pick them up at the ungodly hour. "Hi, sweetie," said Ma.

"This is Frankie," she said.

"Hi, dear. I'm Alice. Nice to meet you," she said.

"Hello, Alice, nice to meet you," he said. They waited for Frankie's very important luggage, which never came. "Well, where is it?" Frankie demanded to know from the airline baggage guy, getting an eye from security. The poor guy at the counter could only say, "We'll deliver it to wherever you are when we get it. That's all we can do. It's being traced from San Francisco. It will get here, that's all I can say, sir."

It was very important because Frankie had a wad of cash and coke in one of them, and he wanted, needed it. "Well, come on, dear. They'll deliver it to my house on Long Island," said Alice. Kathy wasn't moved by any of it, just that Frankie needed a fucking line, and they headed out. When they got to Alice's house in East Hampton, which was quite nice, they got some alcohol in him and gave him a couple valiums to calm him down. He was not sleeping, but Kathy and her mom were, and they left Frankie on the phone to Ripley, whom he was complaining to about what was happening until he nodded out on the phone on the couch. Needless to say, being good friends, Rip and Judy were fairly concerned about Frankie. A knock on the door finally came. Alice answered it; the luggage had arrived.

Frankie's friend, Dockta Rickie, from Sanctuary and Watertown fame, was back at Cambridge, going to medical school, and was coming to Long Island.

He picked Frankie up in East Hampton for the ride back to Manhattan in his new BMW 320i, while they would meet Kathy at Alice's apartment on the East Side later. He was trying to impress Frankie with his new car, and he did when he let Frankie drive, just like back in the good old days. In the madness that was New York City, high performance was an advantage. They played the Pretenders tape at high volume, "Brass in Pocket" and "Stop Your Sobbing."

New York City—this was going to be fun. The first thing he did was go to the best clothing store and have a black velvet suit made to go with his very high-heeled stacked leather Italian shoes, black, of course. Punk? What was that?

Alice was Kathy's nice Jewish mom but also a high-powered PR woman with many well-known clients, such as Bobby Fischer, the chess player, and was well to do. She had been married to a Jewish mobster in Chicago who was clipped back in the day, right after Kathy was born. She was, needless to say, still connected.

Dying to go out in New York City, Frankie got Kathy, who knew her way around, to go out and check out the scene. He wanted to know where every club was to dance and drink. It was party central. After about midnight, Kathy had to work and couldn't hang, so it was Rickie and Frankie. The city that didn't sleep went on and on; the party would never stop. After hours really meant the sun coming up. You'd get breakfast maybe and end up at the Nursery in the East Village and continue drinking.

Once recovered, Rickie went back to Boston. Frankie, Kathy, and Alice went out to a four-star French restaurant. With Frankie's stash gone, he had to cop some coke from a guy Kathy knew in town. The guy had a huge midtown apartment on about the fifteenth floor. He'd never seen anything like it, living large in New York City.

Next stop was Michael the stockbroker's not girlfriend but a girl he knew. Frankie met her at her place. Katie lived in the East Village in what looked like a typical East Village way—a bunch of roommates (mostly women) and a college feel to their roach-infested apartment in which every square inch was in use. It was the opposite from the guy in midtown.

"So, Katie, can I take you to lunch? And I'm looking for a hard-to-find record," said Frankie.

"Sure, I'd love to have lunch with you. And I do know all the record stores. We can see if we can find it," said Katie. After lunch at Ratner's on Lexington, they hit the record stores.

"What's the name of the artist?" asked the guy at the store.

"Klark Kent," said Frankie.

"Never heard of him," said the guy, like the previous five or six record stores did.

"I know a place down on Fifty-Sixth Avenue," said Katie. Finally, in an obscure cluttered underground vintage record place, there was a guy who didn't look at them like they were from Mars for asking and said, "I love Stuart Copeland. Isn't Kinetic Ritual the best song you ever heard? I got a couple. They're very rare, hard to find," he said. "Eight bucks."

"Great." Frankie bought one. "Thank you, Katie," said Frankie, and they went back to her place to listen to it a couple of times. "I have to get back to the east side. I'm leaving for Tampa tomorrow."

"Going to see Junior, huh?" she said. "Well, I had fun. Wish you had more time," she said with a pouty look, like she wanted something else.

"I'm sure I can stay for another half hour," said Frankie.

"Good, there won't be anyone here for another hour," she said. There was not enough room in the improvised bunk system to really spread her legs, but they managed to fuck with abandon.

Kathy and Alice were charming hostesses. He thanked them for their hospitality and was off to LaGuardia, where he barely made his flight, and was off to Tampa, where it was eighty degrees.

"Frankie, you made it," said Junior when he picked him up at the airport. It was eighty degrees, and then it started pouring rain.

Good thing his front-wheel-drive Cadillac, which he was driving at a high rate of speed through huge puddles of water that couldn't even be seen, was able to navigate while he talked about pussy mostly. He was a kind of big guy, jock, good-looking enough, rich, and his thing was asking chicks to "show me your tits."

"Yeah, Katie, she's got nice tits."

"Yep," said Frankie.

"Time for a drink," he said. "You brought some coke, I hope," he added when they took a seat down at the bar.

"A little," said Frankie. He knew that was coming. "A couple of grams."

"Oh man, I was hoping you were going to bring more than that," said Junior.

"A lot of hungry nostrils in New York," said Frankie, aware that it was mainly his two that were the hungriest. They were in a beautiful condo with nice palms and tropical plants around a big pool in the middle of the complex on the beach. They had no sooner gotten there and were pouring drinks when the door opened and in walked a very tan and very pretty brunette with a bikini top on and a towel around her bottom. "Hi, I'm Tammy, a friend of Junior's. He told me you were coming," she said as she held out her hand and gripped his.

"Hi, Tammy, pleased to meet you," he replied as he put his hand out, palm up, and shook her small hand.

"Don't you look cosmopolitan," she said. He was down to a vest and dress shirt with rolled-up sleeves while everyone there was in either Hawaiian shirts or tank tops, shorts, and sandals.

"Tammy's going to be your guide around St. Petersburg," said Junior. "You got clothes? If not, there are some things in the extra bedroom you can wear," he said.

"Thanks, Junior. I think I got everything I need," said Frankie. He went up to Junior at his bar and gave him the two grams he had with a look of "Sorry."

Dressed in the correct Florida attire, they took Junior's Cadillac to St. Petersburg. "Saint Pete is the fourth largest city in Florida with primarily a population of retired people from up north, New York, and Jewish, to be specific. No doubt the reason we have the

Holocaust Museum." She pointed this as they drove past. "We have the Salvador Dali Museum with the largest collection of his work," she was saying as Frankie said, "Yeah, let's see that!"

"Then we'll go down to Baywalk and have a drink."

"Sounds good to me," said Frankie.

"Your wish is my command, Mister Cosmopolitan," she said.

"How was the tour?" asked Junior upon their return to the condo.

"Great, Tammy is a first-class tour guide," said Frankie.

"Glad you had a good time. Let's get ready for dinner," said Junior. "You're going to love this place."

They went to a classic Florida restaurant from the '50s with all kinds of exotic plants and a Caribbean motif, patronized by baseball and football players, golfers, and wealthy retired cotton tops. It was the hot spot in Tampa.

Back at the condo, Junior retired, leaving Frankie and Tammy in the living room kissing and caressing. He was especially taken by the body, really tan and having never taken off her top at the beach. Nice. She wanted him as much as he wanted her, it seemed. "Let's go to bed."

"I'm not going to sleep with you," she said.

"You don't like me?' he said with surprise.

She was just making out with him, leading him on, acting like she wanted it. "I think you're a great guy, but I can't sleep with you," she said. They slept in the extra bedroom in separate beds. She was naked with extremely white breasts, glowing in the dark, and a tan smoking body. "I wouldn't ask you to do anything you don't want to do," he said. He didn't need pussy that bad. He wasn't exactly sure what she was doing but let it be and slept.

Junior drove through the Monsoon at ninety miles per hour. It was like they were in a boat, which they were, and it didn't faze Junior; he was talking about pussy—never mind not being able to see where they were going. They got to the airport.

Safely in the air, in a DC10, which was just about empty, Frankie was glad to be going home. Back to long alcohol and cocaine-fueled binges that kept him from having anything to do with other people, probably talking bullshit to some uneducated nasty slut, happy anyone was paying attention to her. Thank God.

Almost alone on the plane, across from him, a lovely blonde, a professional-looking working woman, sat studiously working on some sort of paperwork. He also had his own writing to do—the *New Wave or No Wave* script. His pen exploded at thirty thousand feet, getting ink all over his professional, hip styling uniform. Not cool. An ink stain—not good.

He couldn't help himself. Sitting there in her gray suit, he approached her and asked if he could sit down. There was no one else on the plane. She said, "Yeah, sure."

After clarifying the ink was a result of opening an unstable pen at thirty thousand feet and not to do that again, they got to talking about her journey and his.

She was definitely a hot piece of ass, all professional and everything but smoking. He knew how to handle these types. Treat them normally. Didn't have to do anything. Just be yourself.

"Going to San Francisco on business?" he asked.

"Yes, I am," she said.

"What kind of business are you in?"

"I work for a French bank in Panama. We have an office in San Francisco," she said.

"A French bank in Panama, that's interesting," he said.

"What about you?" she asked.

"At the moment, I'm a television producer," he said.

"Oh, what's that like? Sounds interesting," she said. "Tell me about that. What does a television producer do?"

"I think working for a French bank in Panama is more interesting. I asked you first," he said. She smiled at his playfulness and proceeded to tell him that the French bank did not report the transfer of funds in Panama to anyone. She spoke French and Spanish and got a favorable mention from Frankie about how smart she looked in her suit. Therefore, ill-gotten tronies, like drug money, could be put into a Panamanian bank, and other than paying Pineapple face (Manuel Noriega) his fee, there was no tax and it could be withdrawn anywhere. He found all this out in a matter of time, but that was the bottom line. "Your turn," she said. He proceeded to tell her he was a producer, promoter of the new and cool, albeit loud, angry, music and was doing a story on it. They needed him because squares didn't have a way to find out what this new phenomenon was about. He realized as he told her that it was, in fact, pretty cool, creative. He liked being someone that knew something other people needed.

"So where are you staying?" he asked her.

"I don't know yet," she said.

"You can stay at my place," he said.

"Okay, that'll be fine. I'd like that," she said. He wanted to fuck the exotic beauty but could not find a way to pull it off, and she wanted him, he could tell. At the airport, he was greeted by Adrianna and Mimi, who were waiting, not too surprised, knowing Frankie, when they saw the tall attractive blonde accompanying him off the plane.

He introduced them. "Madeline, Mimi, Adrianna."

"Hi, hi," they said to one another. Women, always gracious beings. Frankie was very lucky for being such a fool. They delivered Frankie and his guest to his house. It was assumed he was going to do her; Mimi had a new boyfriend anyway, and Adrianna just came to see what was next for its entertainment value. They didn't even know Milly.

They delivered Frankie and Madeline to his house and said goodbye. Mimi was over it with Frankie and had a boyfriend anyway. She may have still been carrying a torch for Frankie, but the event cinched the deal that it was over between them, even though they would remain friends and would meet at motels and safe houses to do coke, get crazy, have kinky sex, and take some pictures.

He got Madeline into the attic, and she was willing and able, but Frankie, so preoccupied, really didn't get around to giving it to her. It didn't affect her one way or the other. She had work and was plenty entertained just to watch what was going on. She was rich by Panamanian standards. She lived next door to Roberto Duran, the famous middleweight champ with "fists of stone." Being a god in Panama, he drove through traffic lights and pretty much had his way with the people. He ran the place, Panama City.

French and beautiful, she knew she was wanted but didn't take any of it too seriously. Frankie, it so happened, was too busy and too fucked up to make it with her. Not a big deal, but it was a waste of effort. Not good that he was too fucked up to function normally. The drug intake was such that it didn't help get what he should have wanted; it inhibited it.

"Want to do a line?" he asked her.

"No," she said. That should have been a clue, but he didn't get it. He mentioned to John Dean that he knew the woman who worked for a Panamanian bank that laundered money, and since his money was black, he put them together. He cut a deal with her, and she was able to launder a couple hundred grand for him. He didn't even get a fee, nor was he screwing her for breakfast, lunch, or dinner, which was what would have normally been happening had he not been such a useless drug addict.

Glen and Frankie got to work on the documentary. A very talented graphic artist at Circle 7 put together a brilliant montage of posters and art (including hockey puck girl) and images of the wild world of Punk with the Klark Kent music (not that it was really Punk, he just liked it) as a backdrop. More self-appointed authorities on Punk were interviewed (such as filmmakers, underground newspaper publishers, and editors). It was enough to do a two-hour show instead of a half an hour. It was going to be a masterpiece.

The work was going on at the offices of KGO with Glen and Jerry. That meant Frankie and Glen were meeting him in restaurants and bars. All the high-end places in downtown San Francisco were well known by the City Hall, and professional and legal people frequented there to get lubed or get right. Lots of wine and calamari. Jerry was a great guy. Happened to be gay, which meant he was connected, liked coke, and liked to drink. They would be drinking and doing coke all afternoon, then at about 4:00 p.m., he would get up and say, "Gotta go do the news now," go get a cab back to the studio on Golden Gate Avenue, get made up, sit down next to Van Amburg, and somehow do the news, live, with a big smile, looking as straight as an arrow. Whew.

New Wave or No Wave finally got the in-studio presentation from Jerry. He was sweating profusely in the Bayscene studio (presumably from maximum alcohol intake, finally revealed, and had to have makeup wipe him down and powder him). The voice-over script and the final edit were in the can and scheduled. Frankie realized Glen had to sanitize it and put his signature on it, but it did manage to stay Punk in its essence. It still had a curl of the lip. Frankie was proud of it.

Hop had been to Thailand, which he would go to and knew well, and bring back smack in his ass. He was getting rid of it through Frankie and trading it for coke. Frankie did a little bit but wasn't the least bit interested in it, nor did he realize how pure it was. He wasn't connected to what was going on in the street as far as smack was concerned, so he sold it to a few connections he did have who wanted it, and one of them was Billy, in Marin, who now lived in a dark apartment on a ground floor of a house on Mount Tam on the ocean side, with no view, right across from Jeanette, who had the view. He got an ounce, and his young girlfriend whom Frankie barely knew, liked it a bit too much. She was kind of sneaking it from him, as he understood it, but OD'd. Died. Billy got brought up on charges but got off with a high-priced lawyer.

That was a wakeup call because Billy and Frankie did quite a bit of business. Billy always had the best coke. Frankie recalled a time he was going over to his house late at night in the worst storm of the year. Stuck on the Golden Gate Bridge due to a head-on collision at about the North Tower left Frankie in his MGA, stuck midspan. The torrent of rain was blowing upward for two hours. It was said that the bridge can swing twelve feet both ways. He sat there swinging back and forth on that bridge. What he would do for cocaine, he thought, while sitting there, swinging back and forth. People would die for drugs, he realized. It wasn't pretty.

Nor was the later part of 1978 when Dan White shot and killed Mayor Moscone and Harvey Milk, the first gay supervisor of the San Francisco City Council. Dan was mad that Moscone didn't reappoint him to the board after he quit in a snit and blew the two away, also making it a hate crime. Keith Moon OD'd, and Sid Vicious tried to commit suicide at Rikers in New York. He was kicking smack, poor boy. Jim Carroll wrote *Basketball Diaries*, a tale of a teenage junkie in New York City who played basketball—thrilling. Punk literature had arrived. It was dark.

To be continued…

About the Author

Capp moved with his young family to Sacramento at the age of 3 from Hood River, Oregon, where he was born in 1953. As a kid growing up during the arrival of The Beatles to America, the war in Vietnam, the protest to it, the assassinations of Robert Kennedy and Martin Luther king, the cultural revolution, the Haight Ashbury, the introduction of LSD, changed the world. Fortunate to have received an excellent education, well-armed for survival, was drawn to Berkeley, ground zero, where his real education began. In the later part of 1969 he moved to Boston as a runaway and transformed himself into someone much older. Finding a home in a church sponsored institution assisting runaways and people who were unable to handle the drugs they were being given got a job as a counselor having had a great deal of first hand experience with these issues. 1971 in San Francisco was a party just getting started where he was a dedicated follower of fashion by night and an apprentice cabinetmaker by day. Always the student, his interests range from art, literature, politics, philosophy, anthropology (cultural and physical), sports, genetics (eugenics). Cabinetmaker, carpenter, general contractor to Berkeley/ San Francisco architects, custom home builder in North Shore of Lake Tahoe, Restoration Specialist of historic buildings, story teller.